B
527C
7989

MW01235126

{Min. Garfield}

TIME TO SET
THE CAPTIVES FREE

How to Start a Deliverance Ministry

Kathy DeGraw

WESTBOW
P R E S S
A DIVISION OF THOMAS NELSON

WestBow Press books may be ordered through booksellers or by contacting:

WestBow Press
A Division of Thomas Nelson
1663 Liberty Drive
Bloomington, IN 47403
www.westbowpress.com
1-(866) 928-1240

Because of the dynamic nature of the Internet, any Web addresses or links contained in this book may have changed since publication and may no longer be valid. The views expressed in this work are solely those of the author and do not necessarily reflect the views of the publisher, and the publisher hereby disclaims any responsibility for them.

Cover design by Christine Minzlaff.

ISBN: 978-1-4497-1115-3 (sc)
ISBN: 978-1-4497-1114-6 (dj)
ISBN: 978-1-4497-1113-9 (e)

Library of Congress Control Number: 2010943528

Printed in the United States of America

WestBow Press rev. date: 1/31/2011

A NOTE FROM THE AUTHOR.

All scripture is taken from the New King James Version Bible.

I did not capitalize the name satan. I do not want to acknowledge him even to the point of violating grammatical rules.

Client – The word client is referred to as the person we are ministering to. We do not mean any disrespect to the people we minister to. For ease of writing we choose to address the people we minister to by "client."

This book is dedicated to:

My friend and teacher ~ the Holy Spirit

and

To my family for allowing our home to be used as a place of deliverance

CONTENTS

PREFACE

I did not grow up wanting to be a deliverance minister or what I call a "demon buster." It was not my life long dream or something I was groomed or trained to do like people who come out of a long family line of ministers. I did not grow up knowing about demons at all. I certainly didn't say "God, pick me, pick me! I want to do this."

My calling to be in deliverance ministry came upon me by the Holy Spirit. My husband was pastoring a church when we first felt called into healing ministry. We both wanted to lay hands on the sick and have them healed through the name of Jesus! I can still recall the day and remember the words my husband clearly spoke. He said "We are going to be in deliverance ministry some day." I said "No you are, I am going to be in healing ministry." Several years later I found myself completely sold out to deliverance ministry and doing it full time while my husband worked at a secular job to support us. Here I sit now writing my first book on deliverance and knowing it won't be the last and I am glad to do it for the people it will set free.

How did I start being passionate about deliverance? I am not exactly sure except to say while pastoring we were up against quite a spiritual battle and found ourselves hearing and experiencing unusual things in the demonic realm we were never taught about. We felt God wanted us to change directions in ministry. My husband left the church he was pastoring and we moved back to our hometown. We started attending a Spirit filled church where we would find ourselves learning about healing and deliverance.

As I pressed into the heart of God and worked on my personal relationship with Him, I did everything I could to grow spiritually. I read the scriptures, attended conferences and studied anything I could get my hands on, as the Holy Spirit led. As I grew closer to God I found the Holy Spirit being my teacher. He was guiding me and showing me new truths and deep revelations and yes, it was about deliverance ministry.

The Lord then connected me with a wonderful couple who mentored me for about 6 short sessions on deliverance and let me sit in on what would be my first deliverance session. I believe often God gives us our hardest experiences first in order to fully prepare us for what He has for us. My first deliverance session was a handful! A full blown demonic possession! It took us six sessions to work with this person and each one was unusual but well worth it. Upon completing these sessions the Lord released me to go out and do this on my own with my own team of people.

I soon found myself in my home casting out demons with the help of intercessors. I knew very little about what I was doing except that the Holy Spirit was going to guide me. My first session on my own, was once again, my hardest session that I had experienced in the first year of deliverance ministry. However, I never took my eyes off the goal which was total freedom and victory for the person we were ministering to. The devil lost, he didn't scare me away, but made me more passionate about what I do. Nothing at all compares to the freedom that is on a person's face when you are done ministering to them. When you see them come into your place one way and have them leave totally different.

I love to see the freedom people experience in Christ and am privileged to let Him use me in this capacity. I am thrilled to be equipping a mass army for deliverance ministry. It is my heart, my passion and who God created me to be. As you read this book, pray, plead the blood of Christ over yourself, and bind the enemy from activating in your life and command confusion to be sent into the enemy's camp. Please use wisdom, the kind of wisdom that can only come from the Heavenly Father in making decisions how to effectively deliver people or yourself. Use this book as a guideline and as I always tell everyone, take everything back to prayer, let the Holy Spirit be your teacher and tell you what to take in and what to throw out. He was my teacher and I wouldn't have it any other way! Many blessings to you God's faithful servant!

Kathy

CHAPTER 1

STARTING A DELIVERANCE MINISTRY

There are many aspects to starting a deliverance ministry. In the pages following you will find a step by step guide and detailed information on how to start your own deliverance teams whether in your home, ministry or church. We are available to personally teach and train your teams through our Deliverance Training School. Please contact our office for more details. Our desire is to help establish as many deliverance ministries as possible. The more ministries we establish the more people will be set free.

IS DELIVERANCE MINISTRY FOR ME?

"Behold, I give you the authority to trample on serpents and scorpions, and over all the power of the enemy, and nothing shall by any means hurt you." -Luke 10:19

"And they cast out many demons, and anointed with oil many who were sick, and healed them." -Mark 6:13

"And He said to them, "Go into all the world and preach the gospel to every creature. He who believes and is baptized will be saved; but he who does not believe will be condemned. And these signs will follow those who believe; In My name they will cast out demons; they will speak with new tongues; they will take up serpents; and if they drink anything deadly, it will by no means hurt them; they will lay hands on the sick, and they will recover." -Mark 16:15-18

"Heal the sick, cleanse the lepers, raise the dead, cast out demons. Freely you have received, freely give." -Matthew 10:8

A deliverance ministry may not be for everyone, however according to these scriptures we are all able to cast out demons. Every believer should be equipped and knowledgeable enough about the scriptures to do some basic deliverance. If you are called to share the love of God you will run up against someone who needs some sort of deliverance.

Whether you feel called to your own deliverance ministry, to assist in a deliverance ministry, or start a deliverance ministry in your church, we are all called to do deliverance. Even if you don't want to be in "deliverance ministry" you are going to need to be educated on deliverance, because you will run up against evil spirits on occasion. How do you know if you are talking to a friend or ministering to someone and they start manifesting a demon? What about the times you cast off a spirit of anger, stress or anxiety while praying for someone? Casting off a spirit is deliverance and you need to be informed. God will guide you into what capacity to get involved in. Pray and seek Him and ask yourself, "What is my heart's desire? What is my passion?" God is going to grant you the desire of your heart because most of the time He put the desire there.

I believe everyone needs some basic education to combat the attacks of the enemy. However, hard core demonic deliverance is not for everyone. Ask yourself, "Can I kick off a simple spirit in a prayer session? Does fear rise up in me when I think about the demonic?" I didn't grow up saying I want to cast out demons. The Lord prepared my heart for it over a period of time.

I never wanted anything to do with delivering witches and warlocks and victims of the occult. Now, thru studying these, I see how deceived they are and I am passionate about exposing the lies of the enemy. The deceit these people have entered into makes me want to go into the dark places, the dark regions and deliver these people from the hold of darkness.

What are your intentions and purposes? Don't get involved in deliverance ministry because you are thrilled with the demons and are attracted to the spiritual realm and think it is intriguing. These are the wrong reasons and it will get you in trouble.

In order to be in deliverance ministry you have to be very passionate about what you do. You have to be focused on Jesus and what He did on the cross. He didn't just die for the healing of our body, He died for deliverance from our sins. You have to be passionate about serving Him and loving Him and His people. You need to be passionate about setting the captives free. One of my favorite sayings is "defeat is not an option." With the power of God active in our deliverance sessions "defeat is not an option," because the power of God comes in to heal, deliver and restore. Praise Him!

You need to know that without Jesus you could not cast out one spirit, but with Him and the power of the Holy Spirit working through you, you can cast out every spirit. I have no doubt that a spirit has to go and get out of the person in Jesus' name. You need to embrace the truth, that He does it, not you. You have to be passionate about setting people free, the smile you see on their faces when the deliverance is done, the peace that comes back into them and the joy that comes upon them. There is nothing in the world like setting a captive free and seeing them changed.

I do many things. I am a conference speaker, I teach in equipping schools, I mentor and equip people for ministry, but there is something that is very satisfying for me in the area of freeing people from demonic influence and bondage. I know the victory of the cross has been won, that what Jesus did was worth it and that people are going to live such a better life. We have changed families, started new generations with no family curses and given people a new way of life. There is nothing more rewarding than setting the captives free.

PRAYER

The first step in starting a deliverance ministry is prayer. Seek the Lord through a season of prayer and fasting in which you can clearly hear from the Holy Spirit to determine if it is the Lord's will for you to go into deliverance ministry. Deliverance is not for the faint hearted, it is hard work and once you enter deliverance ministry you are entering the front lines of battle. The enemy tries to take out those who are on the front lines. I rebuke that he will take you out in Jesus' name and I rebuke and cancel all the assignments of the enemy against you for entering this kind of ministry. I stand in agreement with you for complete victory and authority through the power of Jesus. I am trying to show you what you are entering into is serious business and you must be committed to the call if you want to enter this kind of warfare.

Before considering this kind of ministry ask yourself? "Are you prepared for what the Lord wants to do through you? Is your spiritual walk strong enough to be able to fight against the attacks of the enemy? Do you have Holy righteous anger bottled up inside you to use against the devil? Do you know the word of God and have an arsenal of scripture inside you?" You will need these to fight against the enemy. What are you going to do when he tries to take you out? Are you in an intimate relationship with the Lord Jesus Christ? Do you seek Him daily? Are you in a communion so close with Him that nothing can penetrate it? These are the kinds of things Jesus requires of us, to live a Christian life and a life serving Him through ministering to His people.

Do you believe you have received a Kingdom which cannot be shaken? "Therefore, since we are receiving a kingdom which cannot be shaken, let us have grace, by which we may serve God acceptably with reverence and godly fear" (Heb. 12:28). You need to believe "He who is in you is greater than he who is in the world" (1 John 4:4).

Once you have confirmed it through prayer and fasting, that the Father wants you to enter deliverance ministry, you need to prayerfully find many people to support you in this kind of ministry. I suggest having several different people in your life and ministry that support you. Please consider which of the following the Heavenly Father wants for your ministry.

COVERING OR UMBRELLA

If you are starting a deliverance ministry within your church; your church and the leadership will be your covering or umbrella. Please don't assume this, but go to your church leaders and pastor and ask for this covering and union. If you are starting your own deliverance ministry you need to ask yourself, "Does the Lord want me to be under a covering of another ministry or does the Lord want me to be my own covering and eventually a covering to other ministries?" If you need a covering seek the Lord as to what ministry He wants you to have as your covering. Go to that ministry and ask them to pray about teaching, training, mentoring and covering you in this capacity. Speak with them and talk about arrangements as to this agreement and process.

If you feel led to be your own covering or cover others you still need an accountability structure. As you make connections with other ministry leaders they will want to know who you are held accountable to and what the structure of your organization is. They will make sure what you are teaching is credible and what you are doing is not on your own but under the covering of leadership. In this case if you are a 501c3 organization advise them of your board of directors, and tell them about your mentors and the spiritual leaders above you.

ACCOUNTABILITY PARTNER

An accountability partner is a person who you can solely trust with everything you speak to them. This person is going to make sure you are in prayer, worship, bible study and intimate communion with the Lord Jesus Christ on a daily basis, not just while you study about deliverance and activate yourself in ministry. They will hold you accountable daily for living a Christian life that glorifies Jesus. This person will be honest enough to tell you if a spirit of pride, attention, control or anything else is manifesting in your life or ministry. This person is going to make sure you don't go too deep studying about the demonic and keep you in proper balance for studying the demonic and the things of God. Many Christians have gotten caught up studying the demonic in an unhealthy way. The enemy sees that as worship of him and can use it to twist your thinking and spiritual life. Your accountability partner is going to make sure you don't get any evil spirits that attach themselves to you while doing this kind of ministry. They are the person you can go to and share with them that you have just studied something very dark and demonic, had a rough session dealing with demons or that you can admit to them you need a break from studying the demonic or you need a week off from doing deliverance ministry. They are going to hold you in check as to when you are doing too many deliverance sessions in a day or week. They are going to keep balance in your Christian life and deliverance ministry.

SPIRITUAL MENTOR

A mentor is going to be someone God has placed in your life to grow you spiritually and teach you about deliverance. In some cases the Holy Spirit Himself will be your mentor. However, even if you think the Holy Spirit is your mentor, you should always be seeking someone who is spiritually more mature than you to build a relationship with. We need others in the body of Christ. To find a mentor think about who in your life does deliverance ministry, who is more spiritually mature than you, or who have you looked up to? Go to that person or couple and ask them if they would be willing to be your mentor if the Lord leads. Ask them to pray together and get back to you in one week. Let the Holy Spirit lead it, if it is His will He will prepare their heart. Be careful to bind your flesh and not let your feelings get involved. Don't automatically think a certain person in deliverance ministry should mentor you. Don't be aggressive and say "You are going to mentor me" or "I am going to be in your ministry some day." That is a sure check to most people that it is not God ordained. However, at the same time don't be hesitant to ask someone to be your mentor, if they say no, take it back to prayer and move on. The outcome is not your responsibility, only your obedience. I had a mentor for a short season who allowed me to sit in on her sessions and then ultimately the Holy Spirit was my teacher. He gave me supernatural revelations of the scriptures. He taught me my own style and technique for doing deliverance. My husband and I still have a couple that mentors our spiritual walk.

ARMOR BEARER

A spiritual armor bearer is a person who is absolutely 100% sold out passionate about praying for you. This person is going to drop everything when you need prayer and listen closely to the Holy Spirit's direction on how to pray for you. They are going to get information in intercession that will protect you emotionally, spiritually and physically. Your armor bearer will bring back information for you to pray through and sometimes it will be something you haven't yet received from the Lord. Trust them enough with the discernment to pray through the information they are getting. Ask the Lord to confirm their discernment and then act on the information if it is the Lord's will.

Make sure your armor bearer is someone you can trust and someone who doesn't get their flesh involved in decisions. You need someone to cover your back in prayer while you study and start a deliverance ministry. You need the blood covering and someone to pray against the attacks of the devil. Find yourself someone who is absolutely in love with Jesus, who believes in what you do and who you are. God could have already planted the seeds in their heart to do the job. God turned my best friend into my armor bearer eight years after meeting her.

INTERCESSORS

Every deliverance ministry needs a team of intercessors. There should be two people interceding with you in all your deliverance sessions. This covers you in prayer, helps stir up the gift of discernment and knowledge and pleads the blood of Christ over you, the team and your client.

It is important to have adequate prayer covering when doing deliverance. You should never do deliverance alone. You need assistance as you never know what you will be dealing with. When I was forming deliverance teams I was also forming ministry teams so I took the people that God had already put in my path and asked them who was passionate about deliverance. These are the people I put as intercessors on my team.

Intercessors can also be trained to operate in other capacities on your team. Intercessors can pray in English or the spirit (tongues), they worship, deliver words of knowledge, discern additional spirit names and blockages people might have. I do prefer my intercessors pray in the spirit during the sessions at a low whisper voice so as not to cause confusion and distraction during the sessions.

TEAM LEADER

Every team should have one designated leader, one leader in training and one intercessor when at all possible. In each session try to have one person who can give you an accurate discernment. What we do is deep hard core deliverance, therefore I want to make sure I am adequately covered by my team.

TRAINEES

I allow people who our ministry mentors and have been through our Deliverance Training School to observe and be trained through hands on experience in our sessions. I will only allow one person who is currently in training in each session. I want to be considerate of our client and I do not want them to walk into a room full of people and feel intimidated. I allow our trainees to take notes and ask questions after our client leaves. Since I do not always know the person in depth and their level of discernment I do not allow them to interject in a session.

TEAM DYNAMICS

Work together as a team to set the captive free. We usually have one leader, two intercessors and either myself or a trainee in on the session. We do not allow more than four people in a session and sometimes have gone down to only two people depending on the circumstances and if we are traveling.

Your team can compose of anything you feel would benefit your ministry. Consider who is in your life currently and also pray people in. The Lord will give you the people you need to walk beside you in this kind of ministry. He did for me and I am very grateful!

Prayer: *Father God, I ask that you give these people clear discernment on forming their team. That you affirm in their spirit and send divine appointments and anointed people to them. Holy Spirit please give them a check in their spirit if someone approaches them or they reach out to someone that is not according to Your will or plan. Please confirm in their spirit what level of deliverance ministry You are calling them to and when to start. Father, we put this in Your hands and ask Your will to be done. In Jesus name, Amen.*

CHAPTER 2

STAYING SPIRITUALLY STRONG - PROTECTING YOURSELF

If you are called to deliverance ministry it is important to know that you are not alone. You have the support of fellow deliverance ministers. There are many things that are not talked about but if we are afraid to talk about them, we can't be a support to others in the body of Christ doing this kind of work. My hope and prayer is that by providing you with this in depth information that you will be better equipped to combat the enemy, protect yourself and help set the captives free.

My saying in deliverance ministry is "*DEFEAT IS NOT AN OPTION.*" We are told in the Bible that we have authority over all things. "Behold, I give you the authority to trample on serpents and scorpions, and over all the power of the enemy, and nothing shall by any means hurt you" (Luke 10:19). Jesus has transferred the authority here to us and we need to know our authority to combat the attacks of the enemy. "No weapon formed against you shall prosper, and every tongue which rises against you in judgment you shall condemn. This is the heritage of the servants of the LORD, and their righteousness is from Me, says the LORD" (Is. 54:17). It doesn't mean a weapon isn't going to try to attack, it says the weapon won't prosper. However, you have a part to play in making sure that weapon doesn't prosper. You need to be in an intimate relationship with Jesus Christ and have the power of the Word of God stored up inside you. You need to be spiritually strong and receive this by prayer, worship and being in the Word.

If you are going to be in any type of ministry you must know how to combat attacks of the enemy, how to disarm the enemy's attacks against you. He attacked you as an unbeliever don't you think he will turn up even more heat against you while you are actively and aggressively attacking his kingdom? Absolutely! As you try to destroy the enemy, set people free, bring them to Christ, help them forgive and release the Holy Spirit inside of them, the enemy is not going to like it. He is going to stoke up the fire and come after you harder. You need to know how to combat him and know that the victory is already yours, that the fight has already been won and know that he is not going to disable you.

How do you do this? By staying in the Word, prayer and constant communion with the Lord Jesus Christ. You need to fight the devil with your words and you cannot fight with your words if you don't know the Word of God. You need to be in the Bible daily, stoking up your arsenal. You need to be ready to fight the good fight and take up the sword of the Spirit which is the Word of God. You can't function based on someone else's faith and word, you can't function based on the words that you have heard through sermons and messages. You need to get your own word and in order to do that you need to be reading the Bible daily. How can I effectively fight off the attacks of the enemy if I do not know what the Bible says about protection? God's word says:

"No evil shall befall you, nor shall any plague come near your dwelling." -Psalm 91:10

"For He shall give His angels charge over you, to keep you in all your ways." -Psalm 91:11

"I shall not die, but live, and declare the works of the LORD." -Psalm 118:17

You need to be praying, claiming, stating, decreeing and declaring these scriptures over yourself, family and ministry daily. You need to fight in the offense and be ready with the Word. Don't wait until the defensive measures need to be activated. Football teams who are on the offensive line go through months and months of practice before they get into the game. That is what we have to do. We must build up our offensive line, build up the Word of God within us, so when the game starts, when the enemy attacks we can be defensive in our measures. I love the Word of God, I love to permeate myself in the Word. It is that very Word that helps me to combat the enemy.

There are times during ministry you will hear the enemy or evil spirits in your head talking to you. Think about it for many of you, you have already had a time when the enemy has spoken to you. Think of phrases like "You are no good" "Why don't you run your car off that cliff or into that tree" or "No one will ever love you." These are just a few ways the devil speaks to us. We have all heard him in our heads telling us things that are nothing but lies. The Word of God says in John 10:10 "The thief comes to steal, kill and destroy." All those phrases are things that steal our lives because instead of focusing on the things of God and His promises we are focusing on the lies, getting depressed and sitting on the couch watching TV and eating a bag of potato chips because the enemy has just disabled us. Emotionally, we start becoming a wreck and are too stressed out to clean the house, go to work and advance the Kingdom of God. He wants to destroy your destiny and will try to accomplish this by throwing words and threats your way that will make you rot and stink while you sit and think. You will sit there and think about what the devil is going to do instead of rising up and taking your authority.

Occasionally, when ministering to someone or when I am doing deliverance I will get threats from the evil spirits. The number one threat he will throw at me is "I am going to kill you." He will speak it to me in the spiritual realm or through a person's lips I am ministering to. Immediately, I will rise up and quote scripture Psalm 118:17 "I shall not die, but live, and declare the works of the LORD," and Psalm 91:16 "With long life I will satisfy him, and show him My salvation." I will also rebuke and cancel all word curses and will say something like, "I cancel all assignments of the enemy to steal, kill and destroy, I come against all attacks and assignments from the enemy; I cancel them, consider and call them null and void. I come against and cancel all attacks on my family, ministry and vehicles both now and in the future, in Jesus' name." I rebuke him by taking authority over him with the Word of God.

We cannot let fear rise up against these threats. We know the Word and we know the promises of the Father. He is our rear guard "For you shall not go out with haste, nor go by flight; For the LORD will go before you, and the God of Israel will be your rear guard" (Is. 52:12). If you let fear rise up and stew on what the enemy just threw at you, then you are going to let him steal your destiny, get frazzled and let him steal your time and day. Think about that, how many times have you gotten bad news, depressed yourself by thinking about old thoughts you can do nothing about or let fear rise up about a situation that has not happened yet. What happens? It paralyzes you, you can't think and you sit and think and rot and stink and you don't get anything accomplished. Meanwhile, you added a few pounds to your waste line because you grabbed that bag of chocolate or sat on the couch with the bag of potato chips comfort eating instead of grabbing your Bible and filling yourself up with the Word of God.

I want to share with you how much our God cares about these attacks and what we think. I had never thought much about the enemy killing me. I didn't really take it in but there is something you need to know about me, I don't like to fly. I am not afraid to crash, I know where I am going, but I think subconsciously I may have slightly wondered if the enemy would try to take me out that way. I truly had a spiritual confidence about me and believed the plane was safer because I was on it. I am a carrier of the anointing and would step on that plane, lay my hand on the outside as I boarded and say "Lord I anoint this plane, I thank you that it is safer because I am on it." One time I flew to Colorado and while there ministering had the opportunity to attend an outpouring and I was ministered to.

This man prophesied over me and the Spirit of the Lord said through him "I brought you here tonight to tell you I am your biggest ally, I am your greatest supporter and fan. I am in your corner. Together we make up a majority; together you and I are going to move ahead with your life. Now you faced some things that would have destroyed some women. The devil said "I am going to kill you, I am going to kill you," but the Lord says "I am the shield about you and I am the Glory and the lifter of your head. The enemy that has come against you one way will now flee seven. And just to show you whose boss I am going to let you live to a ripe old age and do the will of God until your very last breath."

Afterward when I got on the plane to fly home there was a little different feeling. More peace came over me as I remembered the prophetic word that I would live a long time and minister out of my last breath. It was so cool because God knew that was the desire of my heart to minister out of my last breath. I don't believe in retirement, it's not in the Bible and not for me. However, my Father cared enough about me to share this prophetic word through someone I didn't even know. How awesome! I love Him so much!

In order to stay spiritually strong you need to watch your backside. After ministering you need to make sure the enemy didn't come in your back door. You have just finished ministering for the day or event and are feeling good about what the Lord has just done. Still be cautious and on guard, these are times the enemy will come and try to attack us, when we are feeling good and think we are living great and everything is fine. He will use these opportunities to sneak in the back door and get into our lives.

To prevent this when ministering in any setting you need to be aware of your surroundings. Take a spiritual inventory as you begin and discern yourself and the atmosphere. Do you have any pain on your body, have you been having a sickness attack you, have you been feeling frustrated or irritated? Do an inventory and know physically, emotionally and spiritually what you are going into a session or ministry time with. Try to handle it in advance, take authority over it and claim your healing, victory and freedom. Do an emotional, spiritual and physical inventory on your client if you are in a personal freedom session such as a prayer, mentoring, inner healing or deliverance session. Ask them questions like "Are you nervous" "Did you sleep well" "Do you have any physician diagnosed illnesses" or "Do you currently have any pain on your body?" In a ministry session by doing a pre-inventory you will know if you have any additional warfare to combat at the end of the session.

Upon completion of ministering to people you need to be on guard because the enemy could try to come in and steal, kill and destroy and interrupt God's plan for your life. He is going to try to distract you and may try to prevent you from being focused and heading in the direction the Lord wants you to go. He is not happy with what you have just accomplished in the other person's life through the Lord Jesus Christ. The enemy is going to try to come and attack you afterward, now I rebuke that in Jesus' name, I am not claiming it or putting a curse on you for an attack of the enemy. I am simply speaking the truth. If you think you can advance the Kingdom of God and not get some heat from the enemy you need to think again.

It is easy to combat the enemy for these attacks because he will use things that are familiar to you, past struggles, addictions and behavior patterns. First of all, recognize the past attacks, become familiar with them so when he tries to throw them at you again you can instantly rebuke them, take authority over them, recognize them and expose the enemy for the lies he is trying to throw at you.

One of the ways we do this is by what we call exposing the enemy. My friend and I will know the enemy is attacking us by using a familiar strategy. As soon as we recognize it we get out our phones and text message each other by saying "ee" which stands for exposing enemy. After the "ee" we put what he is attacking us with such as lying, irritability or whatever his current tactic is. That way as an accountability partner the other person can be praying for us and we have just exposed him. By exposing the enemy you are taking your authority over him, acknowledging and exposing what he is trying to do and most of the time the attack releases the moment we send the text, pray or cast the attacking spirit off.

Another common attack is causing family dissention. If you notice things being off with your family ask yourself "Were things fine in your family? Were you and your husband in spiritual unity, getting along and loving on each other? Has the atmosphere in your home now changed? Are you irritable, letting little things get to you or did you have a recent argument?" Recognize that if you are in marriage ministry and helping people that the enemy is going to try to attack your marriage. He is going to try to discredit you and your testimony so you won't have credibility to share with people you minister to. The neat thing about it is that it usually leaves you with another testimony of how you overcame it. Try to recognize if there are clear differences in your life for the week before you ministered versus after you ministered.

There are some spirits that are very easy to discern. Pay attention to the words you are speaking, what do they have in common? Do you all of a sudden feel frustrated with everyone? Are you frustrated by not having enough time in the day, frustrated with your children and frustrated with your work? Have you been speaking out of your mouth "I feel frustrated"? Here you have just discovered you have been attacked with a spirit of frustration. During or after the ministry time the enemy came and snuck in what I call your "back door" and gave you a spirit of frustration. It is very simple to get rid of. Speak out, "In the name of Jesus Christ I command an attacking spirit of frustration to leave." I will usually feel it leave with a little jerk of my body. I will then ask the Holy Spirit to come in and fill that place. If you still can't get a release call over someone experienced in deliverance prayer and have them pray with you.

If you are still not obtaining freedom see if an old behavior pattern, thought pattern or habit has started to activate or bother you again. Did you struggle with overeating, comfort eating, or smoking? Are these things trying to attack you again? Are you noticing yourself eating more or struggling with a past bondage or having a cigarette craving? You then need to take a step back and discern if the enemy is using one of your past crutches to get you entrapped and ensnared in him. If so command your appestat control center of your brain to come into alignment with the Word of God to control your eating habits. Command spirits of nicotine, tar, smoking and addiction to be cancelled and to depart now in Jesus' name.

Have you had a challenge in the past controlling your thoughts? Are you going back to a perverse way of thinking, are you getting depressed or thinking old thoughts you have conquered? Refuse and renounce to participate with these thought patterns in anyway. Ask the Lord for forgiveness if you have opened the door in any way and say, "I renounce any attempt of the enemy to have these things come back onto my life and I repent of any part I may have contributed in this." Claim scriptures over your life such as:

"And do not be conformed to this world, but be transformed by the renewing of your mind, that you may prove what is that good and acceptable and perfect will of God." -Romans 12:2

"But we have the mind of Christ." -1 Corinthians 2:16

"Bringing every thought into captivity to the obedience of Christ." -2 Corinthians 10:5

Be aware of physical sickness that attacks you soon after ministering. Immediately, at the first onset take authority over these symptoms. A common tactic and often first symptom of physical attack is a dry annoying cough. It can feel like it is attacking your respiratory system, don't take it in. Don't allow him to bind you that you are going to get sick. Instantly start commanding your cough to leave in Jesus' name. Speak aloud "I command all attacks of the enemy to cease to exist in Jesus' name. I command the enemy will not steal, kill and destroy. I rebuke and renounce sickness and disease in Jesus' name." And according to Gal 3:13 "Christ has redeemed us from the curse of the law, having become a curse for us (for it is written, "cursed is everyone who hangs on a tree")." The enemy is going to try to throw fire at you every chance he can and you need to fight fire with fire. Fight the fire of the enemy with the fire of the Holy Spirit. "Because He who is in you is greater than he who is in the world" (1 John 4:4).

A symptom of a demonic attack against your body can be discerned in your body temperature. In order to expose the enemy I want to talk about cold chills after ministering. They are what I label as demonic chills. When you have really ticked him off and done some serious damage to his camp beware and watch out for the cold demonic chills, they can set in within 1-4 hours. They are piercing cold and you will feel like you are getting the flu but you are not. You feel like you are cold to the bone. Take your authority and have someone pray with you if you ever feel these coming on. It won't help to put on warm blankets or more layers of clothing, you need to rise up and fight with prayer and the Word of God. Fight hard, push through it; give it all you got to be victorious. I have also found the best way for me to combat this along side prayer, worship and the Word is to get in a piping hot bath. Get it as hot as you possibly can until you are close to having a layer of skin peel off and then pray, worship and fight from the bathtub. Afterward, go to bed and throw all the covers on you and continue to fight. I have always said ministry is hard work. I feel like a hot tub should be a tax deduction for ministry workers because let's face it, sometimes our bodies feel torn, battered, beaten and bruised when we are done ministering. I rebuke our bodies feeling that way in Jesus' name, but I do think a good hot tub with some praise and worship music would be awesome! I am claiming it and calling it forth!

The last thing you need to be aware of after ministering is heaviness and fatigue. A common tool the enemy uses to wear you down, make you give up, get frustrated that nothing moved forward and that the people didn't embrace your teaching. It is satan's goal to wear out the saints and he will try as hard as he can. As you recognize and renounce the activity in your life he will not have victory.

You need rest and to be refreshed and filled up after ministry. Every time Jesus was done ministering, He went away by Himself to be with the Father. He went away, prayed, refreshed, refilled and basked in the presence of His heavenly Father. When I am finished with a couple of long days of deliverance, traveling out of state or just had a conference, I write in my calendar the following day "Kathy's day off." I take the day off, I don't work, I don't write and I don't answer the phone. I spend 6-8 hours in my living room which is my quiet place and I sleep, soak, sloak (which is sleeping and soaking combined), pray, study and worship. I listen to the Holy Spirit's leading and direction of how He would want me to spend the day and I rebuild for the next time. I grow spiritually and spend the time being intimate with the Lord. We need to enter into a place of rest where He can deposit into us. If we can quiet our minds and focus on Him and just soak, relax and receive He can deposit more into us to pour out next time.

I pray the Lord will help hold you accountable to being with Him and in the Word. I pray all attacks of the enemy would cease to exist in Jesus' name. "For God has not given us a spirit of fear, but of power and of love and of a sound mind." -2 Tim 1:7

Prayer: *Lord, help us to rest in Your presence. Help us to focus on You and Your glory. Convict us Holy Spirit to rest and refill and worship You. Thank*

You for being our comforter, guide and protector. Thank You that we have victory and authority over all things. We love you Jesus and it's in Your name we pray. Amen.

CHAPTER 3

FORMING A TEAM

The following format has worked for me in establishing a quality team of dedicated Spirit filled believers passionate about serving the Lord. Take these guidelines and consider what you need to build your team.

TEAM

Pray in people who are absolutely passionate about deliverance ministry. I have found that most of my team has formed from people I myself have delivered. The people who have had the greatest deliverance are the ones most passionate about setting the captives free because they know what it is like to be bound and then freed. They love seeing the look of freedom on a person's face and the smile of exhaustion that comes at the end of a session. They love defeating the devil and have no fear about combating him.

Pick a team led by the Holy Spirit and pray through every person who says they are interested, not everyone is meant for deliverance ministry. Interview your team and ask them why they are interested and what they want to do. Specifically, do they want to intercede, be trained to be a leader or use this training ground to start their own ministry.

Have people interested in volunteering fill out a form and upon receipt take it to prayer. I have enclosed a sample form in the back of this book.

Interview the person and spend time getting to know them and their heart for the Lord. If after prayer the Holy Spirit releases them into your team allow them to start sitting in on your sessions. A person on our team will start as an intercessor and by observing. We slowly integrate them into the process. Be cautious in allowing someone to come in and start inputting in your sessions until you know they are accurate in words of knowledge and discernment. Slowly integrate them so that you can get to know their heart and the purity they have in serving the Lord.

MANDATORY DELIVERANCE

When the Lord sends us people to assist us with deliverance no matter the level they are assisting us in, they are required to go through a mandatory deliverance session themselves before they can start assisting. If they have previously had deliverance from another ministry they must go through deliverance with our ministry. We expect nothing but the best and God has called us to purity and spiritual excellence. We cannot effectively intercede and deliver other people if we are in need of deliverance ourselves.

We want to make sure the people ministering with us have had the best and most complete deliverance possible. If they received deliverance elsewhere we may not know the extent of the deliverance they have obtained or they may have received it as a general prayer and not had the complete freedom Christ came to give us. We want to make sure they are spiritually ready to minister.

We believe many times as we grow in the Lord, He wants to take us to a new level, give us even more freedom or peel another layer of flesh off ourselves making us more like Him. Additional deliverance is necessary because often the Lord gives us what we can handle for that season in life. As we grow closer to Him, He takes us to a new level, a new freedom and new cleansing as we can handle more. Glory to God! He isn't done with us yet!

Hold your team accountable and make sure they are walking with the Lord. On occasion our teams are asked to go through a clean up session. We schedule a prayer session and make sure they have not opened any doors to sin, took on any old behavior patterns and habits and haven't taken in an ungodly spirit. God could also want to deal with something with them He hasn't revealed before and we want to allow that opportunity for prayer.

Let's face it we all slack off from time to time in our relationship with God. It is during those times we open doors to sin, unforgiveness and demonic spirits. We need to be staying in a continual flow of the Holy Spirit and not allowing the things that bothered us in the past to affect us again in the present or future. These are ways we open up the demonic realm and activate it. Deliverance is a continual process and we want to make sure our teams have the same freedom we offer our clients.

INTERCESSORS

Everyone in our ministry starts out interceding on the team. An intercessor is someone who prays in the session. They cover the leader, team and client in prayer. It is beneficial to have a consistent team of intercessors. These are people where interceding is their passion and usually these people have no intentions to move forward to a team leader. It will benefit you to have intercessors you can trust and who can work with you on a consistent basis.

TEAM LEADERS

We are called to equip the body of Christ. Be in a constant state of raising people up all the time to be a team leader. Encourage people with leadership skills to start as an intercessor and then move into leading a team. Begin with them observing, interceding and being allowed to ask questions afterward to the leader or director in order to learn, grow and be equipped. During the session allow note taking on how you do things and what they are learning. Afterward discuss any thoughts, misunderstandings or confusion they may have.

At the Holy Spirit's leading and as trust and relationship has been built allow them to start inputting in sessions. Use them to give a word of knowledge, testimony or other discernment they are getting. Encourage them to write down on a piece of paper what they want to share or are receiving and hand it to the leader. At that time the leader can discern if it is their flesh wanting to share, a revelation from the Lord or a distraction from the enemy. Always weigh against the scriptures and the Spirit of revelation every piece of information you get. Don't automatically throw it out there. Make sure it is accurate and the Lord's timing.

When you feel the person is becoming mostly accurate with what they have given you then let them start verbally participating in the sessions. Give them freedom to release the information they are getting to the leader or the client. On occasion the leader will get the discernment in advance for all people to be quiet or they will get a check in their spirit if someone is about to share something that isn't pertinent and then we will gently stop the person from moving forward. We are going to occasionally be wrong, we are not perfect, and we are not like Jesus yet. God extends us grace in these situations but we have to put our flesh in check and make sure we are doing everything possible to clearly hear from the Lord.

BUILDING YOUR TEAM

Train a team of people to do what you do. One way we train people is by holding Deliverance Schools around the United States. Our trained teams will come into your ministry or region and set up a Deliverance School where we will come and teach you everything you need to know including hands on experience. We personally require our team to attend these sessions in which they can obtain further training. Visit our website www.degrawministries.org for our upcoming school, to read an outline of our school or to host a school in your area.

BOOKS

We suggest several books for people to study on topics of healing, inner healing and deliverance ministry. It is our recommendation they start out with spiritual warfare books and then progress into inner healing and then deliverance. We have a guideline for every two books you study on spiritual warfare and deliverance to read one on a positive spiritual topic or a spiritual book for personal growth. For example, read two books on deliverance then one book on the fear of the Lord, two books on deliverance and one book on hearing from God. We encourage people to read and study something that will build them up, edify and grow them in their walk with the Lord.

MENTORING

Our team is required to go through a season of individual mentoring with me. I meet with them weekly, bi weekly, or however often the Lord is calling me to during this time of training and building. We talk about their personal walk with the Lord, struggles and challenges they are having. We discuss areas where they need to grow and things they need to learn about. They are allowed to come into these mentor meetings with a list of questions to ask, I answer their questions and we allow the Holy Spirit to move through the gift of discernment to see what He wants to work on in their lives. This is a great time where the Lord ministers to them, gets rid of bondage they no longer need to carry and moves them closer to Him. We close with a time of prayer including casting off any spirits we may discover during the session.

ACCOUNTABILITY

I am consistently checking in with the team and finding out where they are spiritually. I ask them if they have any offenses rising up, if they are understanding what they are learning and if they are still feeling drawn to deliverance ministry. I check in with them about their past spirits they have struggled with along with behavior patterns, habits and other strongholds in their lives. I hold them accountable for the current attacks in their life and see how they are working through it or if they are having difficulties conquering anything and need advice or prayer.

I require the best of them at all times. If I feel they are going through a season in their life where they cannot effectively minister I will withdraw them from ministering for three weeks. Giving them a break from fighting the enemy and the additional attacks they receive through this ministry will better equip them to be able to rise up and fight the enemy in their own life and circumstances. Do not be hesitant to tell a team member, I love you, I care about you and for your well being I need to give you a few weeks off or have you hold off from ministering until you are through this season in your life.

EQUIPPING YOUR TEAM

Train, invest and sow into your team by having them attend Christian conferences with you. Take them and pay for them to go to a place where they can be ministered to. Don't pour out all the time without being filled up in return. We need a time where people can minister to us so we can more effectively minister to others. Invite them to come over to your house and pray and worship with you or study the Bible together. It is so much fun when you sit down with another person and share the revelations you are getting through the Word of God. It's like being a little kid again saying "Look at this scripture, this is what the Lord told me." It is so much fun it makes me feel giddy just writing about it.

I love to pray and worship with team members weekly. Why? Because I love worshiping my Lord. I love the presence of the Lord that is ushered in within the first 20 seconds and I love praying in the Holy Spirit with other believers, what an anointing that comes over you. Hallelujah! Praise You Jesus! Spend time alone with your team by taking them on a retreat and giving them time away with you. During this time plan to teach, pray, worship, study and minister to each of them individually. While you are locked up together discern if they are in need of further deliverance or if they have some demonic attachments. By existing together in a pure environment nothing unholy can live there.

RELEASING A TEAM MEMBER

There will be times in your ministry that you will have to release a team member from serving with you. If you are finding you are having issues with a particular team member I pray a very simple prayer. I do not speak this aloud over them but in my personal prayer time I say "Lord, renew them or remove them." Renew them to have a heart for You and serve You purely through this ministry or remove them from this ministry. The Lord showed me these verses in 2 Timothy 2:23-26 "But avoid foolish and ignorant disputes, knowing that they generate strife. And a servant of the Lord must not quarrel but be gentle to all, able to teach, patient, in humility correcting those who are in opposition, if God perhaps will grant them repentance, so that they may know the truth, and that they may come to their senses and escape the snare of the devil, having been taken captive by him to do his will." The Lord has revealed that if I simply pray the prayer above and abide by these scriptures that He will remove the person from my team without conflict and offense. I have never had to ask someone to leave my team, they have been removed by God through this prayer and these scriptures. Thank you Jesus!

Forming a team takes a lot of prayer, let the Holy Spirit guide you. In 1 Timothy 5:22 it says "Do not lay hands on anyone hastily, nor share in other people's sins; keep yourself pure." It is telling us not to be in a hurry to appoint leaders or even team members. Take it to prayer, don't go out searching for people to serve with you, let the Holy Spirit lead and guide them to you. We want God appointed and anointed people and when we are faithful to Him, He will show us who those people are.

Many blessings and our prayers are with you as God creates your team.

CHAPTER 4

TRAINING A TEAM

In order to effectively establish a team to do deliverance ministry I encourage you to have them attend our Deliverance School. We believe hands-on training is one of the best ways to be equipped. Require your team members and volunteers to come and sit in on several sessions as a way of continuing to train them for what God is calling them to do.

People generally have two different styles of learning. They either like to learn more through the Word of God or more through personal testimonies. Some people can relate more to a life application approach and some people can relate more to a biblical approach. It is similar to how some people can relate more to a teacher and some enjoy hearing a preacher. Since there are different styles and we don't always know what style people can relate to, our ministry leans upon the Word for instruction and guidance. We believe there is a time and place for testimonies and that they minister to specific people for certain circumstances but we like to use them in proportion.

TESTIMONY GUIDELINES

I like to keep balance when ministering and therefore set up testimony guidelines.

- Before sharing a testimony, pray and ask the Holy Spirit if this person needs to hear the testimony and if you should share it.

- Be slow to speak, don't be in a hurry to share your testimony. Make sure you are acting in the Lord's timing and His direction. If He releases you to share it seek Him for the exact timing that it is going to have maximum impact.

- Ask yourself, is this testimony going to benefit the client or do you feel like you just need something to say. Is acting on this testimony going to allow us to get off track, steal time or get us distracted from what the Lord wants.

- When sharing a testimony get to the point. Shave your testimony down by cutting out parts of the testimony that are not pertinent to getting to the facts. Although you may think it is interesting and part of the story you could lose your clients interest if you go too long, don't get to the point or get side tracked on the way.

- No confusion can be present among the team members. There needs to be complete agreement and harmony.

- If you are the leader and know your team's testimonies pray and ask the Lord if they should share it. Don't assume it will benefit the client because they can relate to it.

COMMUNICATION WITH TEAM

Communicating with your team is essential during deliverance sessions. In order to properly build our team up and edify them while training and correcting, I will often speak to them in advance about how I operate and I will review the following guidelines with the team members:

- Any note the leader receives from a team member that gives discernment of a spirit to cast off, a testimony to share or a direction they think we need to go, we are going to discern before we release it into the session.

- Please don't get offended or feel rejected if the leader does not act on your discernment. The leader may be feeling it doesn't need to be addressed now, it is for a different session, it is an opinion not pertinent to the situation or, the enemy is trying to send confusion and distraction.

- If the leader doesn't use a piece of your discernment it does not automatically mean you were wrong. We might not agree with the timing or feel we need to approach it now. The leader will usually tell the team member after the session why the leader didn't feel the release to implement their discernment. The leader will use it as a teaching opportunity.

- The leader may cut you off and say "We don't need to go there" "We don't need to talk about that" or "We need to get back on track." We will even use a hand signal trying to be discreet and cut them off first without speaking the words aloud for the client to hear. If sitting next to each other, we might gently touch the other person's leg as a way to cut them off.

- The leader may ask you to input and talk about what you are feeling. We may invite you to share your revelation or testimony. If they are talking to the person and we feel it is ministering to them, we will encourage them through our words or by a hand motion forwarding our hand towards ourselves for them to continue speaking and sharing.

COMMUNICATION WITH CLIENT

When speaking to a client we need to keep in balance the questions we ask. I give my team the following guidelines when asking questions or ministering to people:

- Be gentle, kind and considerate when asking questions. Be slow to speak and quick to listen to the prompting of the Holy Spirit. Don't be afraid of silence or stopping yourself to make sure you are asking the proper question to get to the solution.

- Watch your word choices and present the question in a Christ like manner.

- Don't sound accusatory, angry or manipulating.

- Do not ask questions out of curiosity or inquisitiveness.
- Try not to intimidate people or make yourself sound arrogant or prideful.
- Be careful not to talk down to people or at them, make sure you are talking to them.
- Show love and compassion in your questions and communication.
- Be real to them and as the Holy Spirit allows speak to them in a way they can relate to.

COMMUNICATION DURING A SESSION

You need to determine in advance for your ministry what is the best way to communicate with your team during a session. We allow for everyone in our sessions to actively participate. Even though we have an established leader they are not the only one allowed to speak or minister during a session. Different ministries function in different ways in this area, you need to establish how your ministry operates. We choose to allow a free flow of the Spirit with order.

When training a person to become part of your team ask them to write their discernment or direction on a piece of paper and hand it to the leader. Encourage the trainee to write down the discernment, what they are getting, a question, a testimony they want to share and hand it to the leader who will accurately discern if this is the time for the revelation.

God has been known to share a piece of information with a team member which is not to be released in that session or ever. We have received pieces of information from the Lord that were helpful in knowing the person, discerning a direction or a fact of something they went through. He has revealed information they may have forgotten about or are hiding from you. Not all this information is meant to be released to the client. You need to be careful what you release and that is why a second opinion or discernment is helpful.

God instantly gives me the word "flesh" if someone wants to share something and it is not His will. In my spirit I will hear the word flesh. Listen to the Lord for what He will give you. He speaks to us all differently. Perhaps you will get a physical manifestation in your body when the discernment is right or wrong such as a tingling sensation or maybe a vision or the word stop. As you seek the Lord and are in fellowship with Him you will learn to hear from Him clearly and quickly.

We communicate by whispering in each other's ear. We generally tell the client at the beginning of the session we may whisper in each other's ear. We are not trying to leave you out or make you feel rejected, it is that we are getting a piece of information and we want to share it with the other person and make sure we are right before we throw it out there and act on it. Your client can feel rejected and fear could rise up easily by someone whispering around them. By telling them this in advance we hope we eliminate some of those spirits from additionally rising up and activating in a session.

I don't encourage you to openly let your team talk and input because if they are wrong it can get the client thinking about what they said. The enemy will use it as a distraction against the client and the team. We talk a lot about dignity and respect of the client. We also want to have these things for our team member. If you shut your team member down in front of other people it can become embarrassing, a distraction and could activate any pride, rejection or offense they have struggled with in the past.

If you feel the need to have a lengthy conversation with a team member from a revelation that needs to be discussed in depth you need to remove yourselves from the room. In this case I will give the client a break, have a team member give them a drink of water and the senior team member and I will excuse ourselves to a different room and discuss the direction we need to take. We keep doors open and make sure we are in hearing distance so we can still keep a watch on what is happening in the room with our client.

We operate together in a session by using physical gestures which I try to teach in advance. These signals can also be used while we are ministering at an event, teaching school, while in a church service or anywhere you need to communicate with your team.

When our intercessors are starting to pray too loud I will take my finger and point down or with a flat hand motion it downward a couple of times. I am not telling them to stop praying, just to lower their voice. When the Spirit really starts to flow and the intercessors are getting passionate about praying sometimes they get a little too loud. This can start to distract those around them, we could have difficulties hearing each other and it can cause a loss of concentration.

I will motion them with my head during a session. When we are trying to get a clear discernment, to determine if the evil spirit is out, we will motion yes or no with our heads. It is conveying to our team whether there is a release to go in another direction. I will also verbally say "Are you good or do you have a clear?" to my team. I am looking at that time for a release from the direction we have been heading or from a particular spirit or series of spirits.

I will put my hand up for them to stop if I feel they are heading in the wrong direction. I mostly stand behind my client with my hands on their shoulders and have my team in front of the client looking at their face and the manifestations. The person cannot see how I am communicating with my team. I do, when appropriate, communicate with my team out loud during a session. I am a teaching ministry and I want to teach deliverance as I do it. I will stop a session or interject something that will further train and teach my team.

We communicate and pay attention to what we feel in the atmosphere and specifically discern if there has been a spiritual shift. If emptiness occurs this could be because the anointing or presence of the Lord has lifted. We could be getting tired or worn out and need some more intercession. We are human and can be distracted by phones ringing, confusion among us or physically not feeling well. I never let a team member who is being attacked by a spirit of infirmity intercede or assist in a deliverance session. If you can pin point the problem or distraction take care of the situation by praying, removing a person from ministering or ending the session if the anointing isn't there to continue.

In the atmosphere we can see if spiritual warfare is taking place. In the Spirit I will see demons and angels flying around battling each other.

In these cases I advise the intercessors to crank it up a notch or we all stop and pray in the Spirit together. We will take authority over what is happening and claim our territory back to the Lord and the session and cover the ministry in the blood of Christ.

If you start to see in the spirit realm demons walking around, crawling around or hiding in corners you should take a break and kick the demons out of the room, out of the building and off the premises. Don't wait until you are done, you don't need them hanging around. Wave around a red worship flag which represents the blood of Christ, anoint the spots or places with oil and get them out!!! Command all evil, foul and unclean spirits to leave in Jesus' name. Cover the area again with the blood of Christ and command all ungodly attachments, defilements and transferences to get off your body, your team and the client in Jesus' name.

I assemble a team that can effectively work together for each session. I do not necessarily keep the same team together all day. We have people come and go all day long. There is balance in this because we get fresh intercession and discernment and people who have been ministering all day can take a break. One strong leader and I will work the entire day together and often feed off each other very well in the spiritual realm.

Every session consists of one leader, one leader in training, one intercessor and could consist of a trainee. Anyone who is not actively ministering to the client will be interceding in the Spirit at all times. Therefore, you have at least two intercessors in each session. After your team is trained I encourage you to have one person who can effectively give you an accurate discernment in each session.

There will be people who are just meant to sit there and intercede and will never move into another position. That is okay, it is where God has called them. We need valuable intercessors. When I minister I want one strong leader and intercessor in each of my personal sessions. That is because what I do is deep hard core deliverance. I want to make sure I am adequately covered. I will only let one person who is training or observing in each session. We want to be considerate of our client and we don't want them to walk into a room full of people and feel intimidated. The maximum we will allow is four people in the room at one time.

The way you train your team is up to you but I encourage you to invest in them. Spend time alone with them to get to know their heart and passion. Always be equipping a leader to be greater than yourself. The more people we can equip for deliverance the more deliverance ministries will be birthed from ours which accomplishes the more people being set free.

"Therefore if the Son makes you free, you shall be free indeed." -John 8:36

CHAPTER 5

DISCERNMENT – HEARING FROM GOD

Discernment is direction and listening, it is obedience and binding your flesh. It is not acting out on what we want but on what the Lord wants. If we want to grow in our discernment we need to learn how to listen. In order to learn how to listen we need to learn how to bind our flesh. Binding our flesh is putting aside what we want, feel or think we should do. It is praying and being open to the Holy Spirit and the direction He wants us to take. It is moving ourselves aside and allowing the King of Glory to come in and work through us.

We increase our discernment by practicing it. By allowing the Lord to encompass us and surround us. It is eating, breathing and sleeping with the Lord being the foremost thing in our mind. I once met a man who was so full of the Holy Spirit it felt like he wouldn't even take a step, a physical step, without asking the Holy Spirit. You could see from the outside that his mind was constantly going in the direction of the Holy Spirit. Even though he was talking to you he was always seeking advice from above.

Discernment is like a chess game always waiting for the next move. I can have my mind totally engaged in a conversation with a person and at the same time be hearing so clearly from the Lord on the direction and next word He wants me to speak out. It is living in a constant communion with the Lord. Your spirit is focused on the Lord and your body is here on earth only to speak the words He would have you speak. When you are in this state of perpetual communion with the Lord, He will increase your discernment. He literally drops or deposits information into your head. It is so unique, so accurate that you cannot doubt it.

When the Spirit of revelation and discernment are in full operation you cannot doubt that it is God feeding you the information to minister to a person or to give you direction for the next step to take. I often wait for His leading and am not afraid to be silent seeking His direction. I do not want to step out of what He wants me to do. I do not want to act in the flesh. I am going to step back and take things to prayer in order to be obedient to Him and to be in His perfect will.

I remember a situation the Lord used to increase my discernment. I was praying about going on a trip with a friend to spend time with the Lord. We were praying about what city we should camp out in with the Lord. As I was praying I kept getting a specific city we were supposed to go to and my friend was getting a different place. Finally I decided it wouldn't make sense to go the city where I thought I was hearing to go. I gave in and decided to go where she was feeling led. The very next day I got a call inviting me to go and minister in the city I had heard to go to. I should have stopped and prayed into it more and not just given in to the other place because it seemed to make more sense. The Lord was clearly telling me where He wanted me to go and I needed to trust him, slow down and wait for it to happen.

Discernment gives you direction and peace, it is trusting God. How can you hear effectively if you don't trust God? You need to trust God so you can trust what He is speaking to you. You can't trust God if you don't know God. You need to be intimate with the Father so you can hear His voice and know His voice. You need to spend time with Him and be in His word so you know what His word says. In this time with Him you will know whether what you are hearing is accurate and according to His word. You cannot know the Word if you don't spend time in the Word. You have to be in His word and know Him so that you can know when you hear His voice whether it is accurate, that it is His voice and not the enemy speaking distraction into your life.

Discernment comes from pursuing a relationship with God, by pursuing Him wholly and pressing into every part of Him. People ask, "How did you get discernment and can you impart it into me?" I received the gift of discernment because as I pursued God, He gave me the rest, He gave me what He wanted me to have.

Are you in hot pursuit of God? I remember a time in my life I pursued Him with everything I had. I read every book, went to every Christian conference, listened to guest speakers at our church and was at church anytime they were teaching something that would interest me, benefit me or equip me for my ministry. I pursued, pressed in, worshiped, experienced visions, had communion with God and you know what happened? It was during that time that my discernment developed and was supernaturally imparted into me.

When I showed God that I wanted Him that He was the thing that I was pursuing, He then gave me the gifts to do the ministry He has called me to do. I am so grateful for the gift of discernment. I love the Lord and I love what He has equipped me with. Can you pursue God? Can you pursue God because you want to, because you desire to and not just for the gifts or what He can give you? Are you in pursuit of the Holy One? Do you want to enter the place of the Holy of Holies? Do you want to be able to be constantly focused on Him? Then pursue His heart, get to know Him, who He is and what His word says about Him. He loves you and wants the best for you.

People pursue the heart of God for the wrong reasons. I never pursued His heart to get something from Him. I pursued His heart because I loved Him and wanted more. I never asked for the gift of discernment. I was never prophesied over that I would have discernment and no one ever imparted discernment into me. It was a supernatural gift from my Father for seeking Him. Now my obedience to seek Him can benefit the many people who I minister inner healing and deliverance to. It can benefit the people reading this book and attending our teaching schools that are seeking the gift of discernment.

With discernment and the seer gifting the Lord can also be preparing your heart and showing you something in advance. I was in a challenging relationship with someone and dealing with a situation where I had to make a decision. I was hoping this decision would be temporary. The Lord was asking me to sever relations with this person for a short period of time. However, I felt due to the person's personality it could end up being a permanent separation. As the months went by I could see things in this relationship that were leading it in a direction I personally didn't want to go. A few days before the relationship temporarily ceased the Lord prepared my heart and showed me another instance where something similar had happened and I made it through just fine. The day the relationship ceased I had a word of knowledge in my spirit and in the morning I spoke out the very thing that happened in the evening. I actually said to someone "You need to prepare my heart because I know this is going to happen." That evening before the person told me they were ceasing the relationship, the Lord had again given me the discernment of what was going to happen.

Did it make it easier? No! I rose up some holy righteous anger against the devil and probably didn't handle the situation the way I should have. I was not happy that this friend who I had mentored and taught everything I knew wasn't taking authority over the enemy's attacks in their life. As I contemplated the next move and how to restore what I could, I was just constantly listening to the Lord. He was telling me to wait and distance myself. It was for my benefit and protection against further attacks and also for the other person involved that they might seek Him through this. There were many times I wanted to text, email, or call the person involved and put my flesh in it. I wanted to get answers and I wanted the restoration process to be accelerated and to just spew some of my fleshly words. I knew that was not the Lord's will. I know one thing for sure, when we wait on His timing, His words, and His direction everything will work out to His glory. I waited, I acted on the discernment He gave me and right now He is restoring that relationship. His timing is always perfect, praise be to God!

We don't have to agree with the way things will work out, we have to be obedient. I have learned He knows things that I don't. He knows what is good for me even when I don't. He knows what I need more than I do. What about you? Do you let Him lead you, let Him guide you, let Him restore you? Do you listen to Him? Take time to listen to Him while you soak in His presence, while you pray, while you walk, while you sleep and always have an attentive ear. Do you hear something? Is it Him? Is He calling you? Is He telling you to do something? Do you hear the nudging of that still small voice? It's Him calling. He is not going to keep speaking to you if you don't listen to His original directions to you. So hurry up and listen, do what He tells you so you can be equipped for all He wants you to be.

How do you function without a strong gift of discernment? You first need to rely upon God and trust Him to give you what you will need for a specific situation. "These things we also speak, not in words which man's wisdom teaches but which the Holy Spirit teaches, comparing spiritual things with spiritual" (1 Cor 2:13). He will give you the words to speak and the discernment.

People have ministered for years without operating in a strong anointing of discernment. In the gifts of the spirit, gifts can be imparted for a specific situation or time. God knows what you need. When you don't have a strong gift of discernment, you need to be praying. You need intercessors along side you to pray with you and give you what you need. When you are talking and ministering to people you sometimes have an idea when words are just flowing out and you don't know where they are coming from or why you said it. This is an instance where the Holy Spirit is just pouring through you and using you for His glory.

Place yourself around someone who is more spiritually mature than you. More experienced people will help you pull out the information. Let them mentor you and sow into your life and ministry. It is important to gain knowledge from other people. You are not in this walk alone, we are all working together to build, edify and set free the body of Christ. As you are mentored in your faith you will learn how to more effectively be the person in ministry Christ is creating you to be.

Don't get frustrated! Frustration will block your discernment and hearing from God. If your mind starts twisting, trying to analyze and figure out how are you going to hear effectively from the Lord, you are putting so much garbage in it by trying to figure it out yourself that you couldn't hear from the Lord if you wanted to. It becomes a twisted plate of spaghetti and even if the Lord stuck the right piece in there you wouldn't know how to get it out because it is so intertwined. You couldn't pull the one piece out without affecting the others.

Don't let pride rise up. People are bound with pride if they don't know the answers or have to say I will get back to you on that one. I don't care if I don't know the answer. I am not afraid to say I am not sure. Our pride can cause us to not minister in the ways the Holy Spirit would lead us to minister to His people.

Test out your discernment. Be bold and start acting on the discernment you are getting. Perhaps it doesn't make sense to you but take a step of faith and see what happens. One time I was ministering to a team member at a retreat. As they were sitting in a chair I felt the Lord tell me to get a small cup and mix oil and water in it. I was obedient and came back with it. When I did the Lord told me to stick two of their fingers in it. I am not sure exactly what happened but the person started weeping and afterward started journaling and then they went home. About a week later the Lord showed me this verse in scripture. "Then I washed you in water; yes, I thoroughly washed off your blood, and I anointed you with oil" (Ezekiel 16:9).

When I asked her about it she said it was one of the most spiritual experiences she had ever had. It was a crucial moment in her receiving freedom in an area of her life and I give God the thanks and praise that I could be obedient with an unusual request. He dropped the word of knowledge and direction into my mind in a gentle subtle manner. At the same time, the remainder of the team surrounded us, praying in the spirit so the gift of discernment was increased.

The first time we receive a new and unusual discernment there may be some hesitation. We may even miss it the first time and not act on what we hear for lack of confidence, fear of man, pride of being wrong or the outcome but when we do miss it we are sorry we didn't try it. We try to step up again, repent of what we didn't do and say God we are sorry but will you give us another chance and eventually He does!

I remember a time where I was assisting someone in bringing out their prayer language. As I was praying with them I felt like their prayer language was on the tip of their tongue. I felt I needed to slap them on the back and it would come out, not hard of course but a simple slap. I didn't do it out of concern for what the person would think. After we ended our prayer session they said "I felt like someone needed to just slap my prayer language out of me." Even God had prepared their heart for what He had wanted to happen. Our God is a faithful God.

If you step up and out in faith, God will deliver. But if you don't take that first step you might not ever have the chance.

CHAPTER 6

PHYSICAL DEMONIC MANIFESTATIONS

"Behold, I give you the authority to trample on serpents and scorpions, and over all the power of the enemy, and nothing shall by any means hurt you." -Luke 10:19

"No weapon formed against you shall prosper..." -Isaiah 54:17

"And these signs will follow those who believe; In My name they will cast out demons; they will speak with new tongues; they will take up serpents; and if they drink anything deadly, it will by no means hurt them; they will lay hands on the sick, and they will recover." -Mark 16:17-18

These are some of my favorite scriptures regarding deliverance. There is nothing to fear with demons because we have been given authority over all things (Luke 10:19) and "There is no fear in love; but perfect love casts out fear, because fear involves torment. But he who fears has not been made perfect in love" (1 John 4:18). Jesus' love for us is perfect therefore we should not fear.

Even though we have the authority there are manifestations of demonic spirits that happen on occasion and we want to educate you on how to handle them. This is a controversial subject and what I am going to tell you is from life experience. You don't have to agree, but I am simply stating the facts and hope by telling our experiences we will be able to help someone else.

There are many ways demons can manifest and although this list is not complete we have compiled the ways in which we have seen most of the demons manifest in our ministry.

These are what I call some of the "symptoms" to look for that a demon might be present in a person:

- Fidgeting in hands
- Pulling of fingers
- Unusual feet movement
- Any unusual distractions
- Compulsive itching
- No eye contact
- Hat pulled down over forehead to cover eyes
- Head slumped down toward ground
- Any uncomfortable movements or gestures
- Hands gripping/pulling each other
- Hands gripping a chair tightly
- Fingers interlocking and unusual finger movements
- Tightness of jaw, jaw appears locked and face around jaw is distorted
- Staring eyes, glassy eyes or bloodshot eyes
- Stomach moving, will look and feel like a roller coaster moving
- Facial expressions and changes, person can look different one moment to the next
- Voice fluctuation or unusual voice tones
- Clenched over, bent over, or abnormally bent backwards
- Appearance of going into a trance or slumber appearance
- Tightness anywhere on body
- Moving pain, pain jumping around their body

The following is a list of ways demons can be expelled through a person or a team member delivering them:

- Blinking
- Sneezing
- Coughing
- Yawning
- Vomiting
- Breathing
- Burping
- Crying
- Screaming
- Seizures
- Twitching
- Shaking
- Stomach movement
- We can feel them leave through us
- We can see them leave
- We can see them go off a person and appear in the room

How do you determine if a demon has left? Look for any of the above items to cease and any of the following signs:

- Eyes will return to normal
- Normal facial expressions
- Be able to effectively communicate with the person
- Feel tired or worn out
- Visual discernment, ask the Lord to show you the spirits in or on them
- Ask a team member if they have a clear, if they feel the demons have left
- Look at above manifestations and see what has stopped
- Ask God for the gift of discerning the spirits
- Ask the Holy Spirit

- Analyze your movements and actions if it went out through you or a team member
- Seer gifting - watch it leave and what is happening
- Do you have a release from praying for this person or spirit?
- Jesus felt the power go out, did you feel the power go out?

TEAM MANIFESTATIONS

What if a team member gets a demonic attachment during the session? If one of our team members feels they have gotten a demonic attachment from the person or an attacking spirit we encourage them to move themselves to the other side of the room and take their authority and kick the demon off. A spirit we just kicked off that person could be trying to find another body to live in or it can be a spirit of distraction trying to disrupt the session. These are very easy to get off and usually the demon will leave once he has been discovered. If we feel it, we will swipe it off the person and simply say get off in Jesus' name. We then will take a moment to say aloud "All demons will go quickly and quietly and will not attach to anyone in Jesus' name."

If the demon still hasn't gone, which is very unusual, I remove the team member from the room. Demons have a tendency to feed on each other and if the demon hasn't instantly left the room it could be because a team member could have opened the door to sin or is still dealing with an issue (because none of us have arrived yet). Therefore, the demonic can feed off the person in the room who is dealing with the same issue. If that is the case, ask the team person to leave the room until you are done dealing with that spirit or group of spirits.

UNGODLY MANIFESTATIONS

There will be times in your ministry in which you will have untimely manifestations of demonic spirits. In this section we will be talking about when an evil spirit manifests in a bible study, during a worship service or a public place. In the event a person starts to manifest a demon in a public event first of all evaluate who you are with and where you are. The number one thing you need to keep in mind is preserving the dignity of your client and the professionalism of your ministry.

If a person manifests a demon in a small group setting such as a bible study or accountability group you need to discern the situation. Ask yourself the following questions:

- "Do I need to address this now?"
- "Is the manifestation severe in which everyone is noticing what is going on?"
- "Am I just discovering a simple spirit attacking them that will subside in the next few minutes?"
- "Do the people in this group believe in the demonic?"
- "Do I have any strong intercessors in this group of people?"
- "Would the person be uncomfortable with their sins being known to these people?"

We are not talking about embarrassment here. That has already happened because they are manifesting demons. The person I am talking about is usually yelling at you, becoming violent or you can clearly tell you are not dealing with the person here but the principalities (Eph 6:12). We want to make sure that if demons start coming out there would not be something that might come up that the person wouldn't want the other people to know about. If you are content with the answers you get to these questions. Then proceed and deliver the person of the demon and command it to leave the premises.

If a person is in a worship service consider where you are at in the service. Is it altar ministry time and the person is at the altar and can get a simple prayer to kick the demon out? Are they manifesting during the service while the pastor is preaching? If the demon is acting out while a pastor is preaching, the service is quiet or it is an inappropriate time and you can tell it is a distraction this is how to approach it.

Approach the person and ask them to come with you. If they don't cooperate, then command the demon to go down and back in the person. I would say something like "I bind you from activating in Jesus' name and command you to go back down and in." Again, when you have authority over it ask the person to come with you and take them into another room. This is done so the demon cannot interrupt the service and flow of things and for the benefit and dignity of the person who is oppressed. After arriving in the other room, minister to them and cast out the demon with an intercessor present. If that is not an available option refer them to a deliverance ministry and pray a blessing over them.

If a demon manifests during altar ministry there are a couple of things to discern. Consider the intensity of the manifestation. Does it need to or have to be dealt with right now? We suggest with strong manifestations that can be a distraction to take them into a separate room for deliverance. We have a team waiting who does not actively minister with us in the prayer line. These people are ready and waiting for demonic manifestations and they will take the client into another room to set them free.

If a person is strongly manifesting and there are many things going on such as worship, prayer lines, etc. and people won't notice you doing some deliverance at the altar, then take your authority and get rid of the demon right there. We have had to deal with manifestations at the altar. Many people are being ministered to at the same time and most times other people don't even notice what is going on. We therefore, command the demon to be quiet and gather our catchers and intercessors around and kick that demon OUT! If it is going to be a distraction take the person out of the meeting whatever that looks like.

Listen to the direction of the Holy Spirit, don't act in your flesh or what you want to do but listen to what He wants you to do. Be gentle and kind to the people and move them to a place emotionally, spiritually and physically where they can obtain the freedom Christ purchased for them at the cross.

CHAPTER 7

ACCEPTING A CLIENT

We receive the majority of our clients through referrals. We also obtain clients through local healing rooms, by people attending our meetings and we receive some people through our website. We get more than enough people sent to our ministry for inner healing and deliverance through word of mouth. You don't need to advertise if you want to do this kind of ministry. The lives that you change and the freedom they obtain will be your advertising.

When someone contacts us for deliverance ministry the first thing we do is send them an application to fill out. We send this application via email or postal mail. With the application we include a cover letter explaining what we do and a legal waiver. These forms can be found in the forms section of this book. Upon receiving the form, we will discern it and make sure the Lord wants us to do their session. We then will contact them with the direction the Lord wants us to take. We will talk later on how to discern if the Lord wants you to do their appointment.

We do not recommend scheduling an appointment until they have returned the paperwork. A small percentage of people will never return the forms and not everyone will call and cancel their appointment. You want to make sure you have people scheduled on your calendar who want to be here. Properly convey to clients on the phone exactly what you do and what your beliefs are so they know what they can expect in their prayer session. This will help avoid cancellations.

As you start your deliverance ministry prayerfully request how often the Lord wants you to do sessions. Consider how often you want to do them, how long you think you should make each session and how much of a break in between sessions you need. My first recommendation would be two sessions a week. Start out with 2-4 hours per session depending on what you think you can handle. I would also suggest if they are four hour sessions to have them on two different days of the week to start. Different ministries have different expectations and lengths of times they do deliverance sessions. When we first started doing deliverance most of our clients were scheduled for two four hour periods. Over the course of learning more about deliverance, growing in our anointing and now having the manifest presence of the Lord enter our sessions we have gone from eight hours to four hours to two hours to now one hour per session.

How can you deliver someone completely in one hour? You usher in the manifest presence of God through prayer, praise and worship. He is the deliverer not us. You call forth the glory to deliver these people supernaturally. Yes, there are times when they may need a follow up inner healing session or you might have done some preliminary work on the client. But glory to God when His presence is there we have had people completely delivered in five minutes. How? We believe! We believe in the supernatural and we expect the supernatural. Deliverance is a miracle and God is in the miracle business. Rely on Him to minister to His people through you. Go with the leading of the Holy Spirit and follow His direction through discernment.

When scheduling multiple deliverances in a day you need to determine how long a break you need to take in between sessions. If you have two sessions which are two hours long, take at least a half hour break. Take into account when scheduling your breaks those sessions can and do run over. You can run up against obstacles, a person could be talkative or you started something you need to finish. If your next client arrives early and your first client ran over, you just lost your break. While you are new at this, plan carefully.

As your sessions decrease in length and your clients increase, you need to determine how best to plan your day of scheduling. In the past, we would plan a half hour in between each session to allow for people who like to linger to get out the door, bathroom breaks, brief discussions on the client and for clients who arrive early. We currently consolidate them much more and are able to keep on our time schedule and gently point out to our clients we have another client waiting.

As you become experienced and strong in the Lord, I recommend what we call "deliverance marathon days." We stack, pack and rack the sessions. We have them back to back all day long with a half hour lunch and sometimes break for 1 hour for supper. We can do anywhere from 5-8 a day. We schedule 1 to 1 ½ hour appointments depending on their circumstances. We break for lunch, however most of the time we don't eat lunch it's just a time to breath, refresh and regroup. Should we decide to go into the evening we will take an hour break (around supper and again no eating unless the Lord releases us). After ministering all day it is a longer time to refill and put in some soaking music. We continue with approximately three more sessions until about 9pm. We then take time afterward to worship, let the Lord minister to us and pray off any attachments and clean the ministry center of any demons that were released. We make sure we are spiritually prepared and strong and have been in the Word, prayer, worship and fasting in order to do these kinds of sessions.

Determine what day, night or weekend day you want to do deliverance and stick to it. We suggest if you are ministering out of your home to pick a day and time where the rest of your family isn't going to be home. In the event you are ministering out of a church, pick a day and time where the least amount of people or activities are taking place in the church. Respect people's privacy, they do not want others seeing they are coming in for deliverance. We generally only do weekday, daytime deliverances and open an evening up for sessions when necessary. This could cause conflicts for full time workers but we also see how serious people are about deliverance. If they want it bad enough they will take the time off work. We refer to it as a doctor's appointment; they will take time off to get physically well they may also need to take time off to get spiritually well. If we cannot accommodate them due to our schedule, we will refer them to another deliverance ministry who schedules nights and weekends. To keep in the spiritual excellence that Christ calls us to, I would only suggest recommending them elsewhere if you know they are a credible source and believe they will go deep enough to set them free. As your appointments increase open up more days of the week to minister and make adjustments as necessary.

We encourage men team members to assist with deliverance on men. Many men come in with spirits of lust and anger. Due to anger, violence, assaults and other sexual harassment issues it is for the safety of all those involved that women do not minister to a man without a man team member present. You don't know the people coming into your center and you want to keep safety in mind. When we experienced an influx in men needing appointments we opened more evening appointments. We had to be considerate and couldn't ask our men team members to take off from work frequently. We opened up two nights a month to do men's deliverances and chose to do it on a night the men were going to be in our place of ministry for another event.

Have scheduled times you do appointments, do not allow people to slide in your schedule. If you do, you have not been spiritually prepared by prayer, fasting and being in the word. The enemy will come in and disrupt your schedule and the session won't be successful. The enemy will also use lack of organization to send you people as distractions, to steal your time and send people on assignment to disrupt. Set up a specific deliverance schedule. If they are God anointed and appointed it will work out.

As the deliverances increased I then kept a balance of when I was ministering elsewhere. I would always look at my calendar at a glance and see what was coming and keep a good balance.

I would make sure I had time off that week and that I wasn't booked with a lot of other activities. I would have open spots in my calendar, but if you truly want to balance and be obedient, you need to book out a couple of weeks and make sure you are staying focused on the things of God. If you do too much deliverance without having a strong relationship with the Lord, you can get your focus in the wrong direction.

For those of you who minister in the home, you need to balance your family. You don't want to be ministering constantly and having your family resent it. You should always put the Lord first, family second, and then ministry. For those in pastoral or church ministry if you are volunteering or serving in another capacity the same week you are doing deliverance, be sure to keep a healthy balance. Don't fill your calendar doing for the Lord and leave yourself no time to be with the Lord. We need to be like Mary and leave ourselves time to sit at Jesus' feet. Keeping yourself in check is our duty as a Christian. Make sure you are spending time with the Lord, not just doing for the Lord.

I do not recommend doing any deliverance before or after a big event. If you are in ministry and you have church services, conferences, teaching schools and other ministry events, try to make it a rule not to do deliverance sessions three days before or after when at all possible. You don't want to wear yourself down spiritually before or after an event, you need to do what Jesus did. When He was done ministering He always went away and spent time with the Father refilling and worshiping Him for what He did. When you are done ministering you are tired and worn out, ministering is hard work. You are in no shape after a weekend away traveling and ministering to come home and battle the devil without first filling up. After traveling and upon arriving home I always take the next day off to refresh and refill. I write in my calendar "Kathy's day off." I spend it sleeping, soaking, worshiping and praying. I refill and refresh with the Father so I am ready to go again.

The only exception I make is when we travel to other states and we specifically group our deliverances and conferences together. I will pray and fast in advance and during the week. We will travel and do a meeting one day and personal deliverance sessions the next. I will keep going for a few days straight, however, when I get home I will make sure I have three days off before doing deliverance sessions. We have also learned when traveling for the ministry to do the event first. After the event we then have the personal deliverance sessions toward the end of the trip. It was taking more out of us physically and spiritually to do the deliverance sessions first and then to try and preach and minister at a conference.

Set your schedule, don't let the enemy dictate it. In deliverance ministry timing is everything. Think about all the times you have looked back and said "That was God's perfect timing or if it would have happened sooner I wouldn't have been ready." Often we get so impatient waiting and wondering if God's timing will ever come to pass. We live in a fast food society and a time of electronic advancement. We are used to having everything at our fingertips and having everything now. In ministry, this can be an obstacle and a challenge.

One thing I have learned to do over the years is to be obedient to the Lord, to the wisdom of His plan and to know His timing is always perfect even if I don't understand. Ask yourself, if you want the Lord to bless it or honor it? If you are waiting on the Lord's perfect timing, when He says go. When the Holy Spirit releases you to do it or when the Lord gives you a specific date to do ministry the Lord will bless it. You will feel the anointing, the glory and the manifest presence of the Lord will be there. If you are unsure or acting out of God's timing, many times He will still honor it. You will feel the Lord there, freedom will occur but you will notice that it isn't as easy as when He blesses it.

Occasionally when you are out of the Lord's timing it will just plain and simply fail. Failing isn't an option for me in personal ministry sessions, lives are at stake. You can cause more harm and damage to someone by having their personal ministry session fail. Let me give you an example. Someone calls up and needs deliverance prayer now. They are begging you that they are in this terrible state of mind and don't know how they are going to get through the next day. They insist that you to take them in the next 24 hours. Coincidentally, they have had this issue or problem for four months or four years. However, suddenly there is urgency in their flesh to get this taken care of when they have lived with it for a long time.

When someone calls up in desperate need that should be your number one flag to take it to prayer and ask the Holy Spirit for His timing. Everyone that calls is in need and everyone who calls we want to help, but we need to lean on the Holy Spirit for understanding. Everyone has a level of desperation, but I want you to take it to prayer when the Holy Spirit gives you an internal check that they are trying to get on your schedule and force their way in as soon as possible. If you are in communion with the Lord Jesus you will know when you answer the phone who these people are. He will lead and guide you into all direction.

When you respond and start scheduling people out of desperation you have just begun to act on the enemy's timing or a person's timing and that is a dangerous thing to do, because then you are not operating in the spirit but in the flesh. You need to realize from the beginning you cannot fit everyone in. There are times the enemy will have them call you to distract you from what you are suppose to be doing. Things such as spending time with your family, refreshing, being with the Lord, writing a book or preparing for a conference. If the enemy sends you someone when it is not God's timing it can interrupt God's plan.

What if you are preparing for a conference by writing a message or studying or praying and fasting and you fit an impromptu session in? It can affect the outcome of your conference. We want God's blessings by being obedient to His timing and will. The enemy can send you distraction after distraction so you never have any free time or get anything done.

What if your mind is so focused on writing your book and He sends you someone to distract you? Did you ever consider the person would be worse off than before if it wasn't God's timing, or if you weren't spiritually prepared and in the mind set you need to be? God can use us where we are, but we need to make sure we are always acting on the Holy Spirit's prompting.

People who cry out in desperation have had their mental illness for a while. For instance, they were bi-polar for 20 years and they call you up and say I need deliverance tomorrow. They have been that way for 20 years! Two more weeks is not going to make a difference. Maybe they have been in a bad marriage and want help right now. What they fail to tell you is their marriage has been shaky for 2 years, but all of a sudden they get desperate and think they need help now. Again 2-4 more weeks is not going to hurt them.

Pray with them, encourage them to attend a spirit filled church or prayer group and schedule them in the time period you need to. Assist in plugging them into a group of strong spirit filled believers until you can see them. We encourage people in Michigan to come to our weekly meetings before and after their deliverance to stay plugged in, encouraged, built up and edified within our body of believers.

How do we communicate to people who are in need of deliverance that we can't help them? There are two reasons we can't help people:

1. We are not the ministry or person God wants to use to help them.

2. This is not the time for any number of reasons or for the simple fact they are not ready to let go.

Let's discuss each of these in more detail.

1. We are not the ministry or person God wants to use to help them. I believe God puts certain people in our path. There are certain people we can relate to and certain people he wants us to help. Think about it a person who has had hands laid on them 10 times for healing and they received their healing on the tenth time. We don't know if they had a roadblock or if God needed to use a certain person or ministry for a certain reason.

2. The deliverance team or leader is not spiritually prepared. The leaders have not been in a time of prayer or fasting, for this reason I encourage you to lead a fasted lifestyle. Ask the Lord to reveal something you can fast from for the rest of your life. I personally only eat meat 3 days a week and the Lord has called me to abstain from seafood, pork and alcohol for the rest of my life here on earth. That is living a fasted lifestyle! I still incorporate other fasting but this way I feel I am always prepared at a moments notice.

3. You, your team or ministry is under spiritual attack. I believe God can use us at those times when we feel inadequate, unprepared and unworthy. However, I believe when possible as mature Christians, we need to be aware of the fact that when we are going through these times we aren't feeling as spiritually strong as we would like to be. Therefore, I believe

the enemy can also use these times to intensify the attack and add more pressure to us if we aren't being led by the Spirit of the Lord.

4. The person is being sent as a distraction on assignment from the enemy. Be careful, the world is full of deceivers. Yes, the enemy can send us people to steal our time, confuse us or curse us. "Be sober, be vigilant; because your adversary the devil walks about like a roaring lion, seeking whom he may devour" (1 Pet. 5:8).

5. To take an appointment not led by the Spirit could overbook your schedule, stress you out, take away from family time or make you cancel another important appointment. Be obedient and listen to the Lord's leading.

We cannot afford that kind of mistake with deliverance ministry. We are talking about peoples' emotional and spiritual well being. If we take them into our ministry and they walk out of here undelivered they are going to feel more burdened, rejected, insecure and heavy. Worse yet, they just exposed their life story, their embarrassing moments and all their sin to a group of total strangers who couldn't help them obtain freedom and victory. We need to be sensitive not only to the spirit of God but to the people of God.

The second reason we might not be released to do someone's session is that they are simply not ready. As much as people say they are ready and willing, sometimes they are not. If it isn't the Lord's timing the session won't be successful. Some people come in with too much unforgiveness they haven't dealt with or have such condemnation, guilt and insecurity you can't break through. You end up getting nowhere because they can't let go and get rid of the fact that their father beat their mother, that their ex-husband abandoned them and the children, or they can't forgive themselves for the adultery they committed.

You try and try to break through to them and to minister to them or deliver them and the bottom line is they can't give up what they are holding onto so tightly because they don't know how. They think their baggage is who they are. They don't know how to identify themselves without it and who they will be if they give it up. It has been a big part of the attention they have received and how they communicate with people. They fear that no one will love them if they don't have this story to tell.

Here are some of the reasons for taking deliverance sessions and timing to prayer first.

For the client the detriment could be:

1. They are so bound by the enemy and their mind is distracted. They are so overwhelmed their brain is like a plate of spaghetti all intertwined and the demons aren't going to come out if you tried.

2. They are in a state of panic and can't effectively hear from the Lord and have so much confusion going on that they wouldn't be any help to you in the session.

3. They truly are not ready for it. They think they are but they don't really believe in it, embrace it and understand the demonic. A friend recommended it because they had an awesome experience and wants the person to feel the same way.

4. It is not the Lord's timing. Often we don't understand why it wouldn't be God's timing for someone to be delivered, but it is not our responsibility to understand only to be obedient.

5. Due to these factors we won't be able to set the person free and therefore will leave them worse than before or, feeling discouraged and rejected and therefore they won't seek help again.

If you start these sessions you will end up getting nowhere in the session and have to reveal that to your client. You explain to them I believe you need to go home and work on the forgiveness issues and whatever else they need to. After going home they are feeling helpless because you, a minister or anointed person of God, can't help them and they feel rejected once again. These people find it very difficult to rise up to seek the help they so desperately need and can end up living that way instead of believing Christ came to set them free.

If you would have stopped and prayed first and asked the Lord, "Do you want me to take this client on and help them?" You would have gotten a "no or wait" and could have simply told them with love, "I have prayed about meeting with you. I would enjoy meeting with you, but I take everything to prayer before the Lord and He is telling me to wait. I certainly believe God has just the right person to minister to everyone. I believe God puts us in the path of certain people for a reason. And currently I don't know why, but the Lord is telling me to wait on ministering to you. So meanwhile, I ask you to pray to the Father and ask Him to put the person in your path that can best help you through the guidance of the Holy Spirit. I further invite you to call me back in 3 months if you haven't received help elsewhere and I will again take it back to prayer and ask the Lord if the timing is right. I know you don't understand and I want you to know I do care for you but, I want you to know I care enough for you that I want you to get the proper help the first time. I know you have been through a lot and I don't want you to have to tell your story over and over. I want God to give you the best person and the right person for your situation the first time so you only have to go through it one time. May I pray with you?" Then pray something like this. *"Heavenly Father, please be with "person's name". Help them to find the proper person to minister to them in your timing. Father God I bind up the spirits of rejection and confusion and ask that you pour your love into them. Give them peace in the waiting period, be their comfort and guide. We ask you these things in Jesus' name. Amen."*

CHAPTER 8

HOSTING A SESSION

When hosting a personal ministry session there are many things involved. I encourage you to take the following and adapt it to your ministry. This is what I have found to be beneficial.

TEAM

Have your team arrive 30 minutes before the first session of the day. Upon arrival they pull the clients application, set up the room and anoint and pray over team members. Each team member comes in with an attitude of prayer, worship, fasting and serving the Lord in purity and spiritual excellence. The team prays for the clients and gathers any advance words of knowledge the Lord would impart to them. Make sure everyone is in a good spiritual place and ready to do warfare. Seek any additional direction from the Lord through prayer.

MUSIC

The team sets up music for the session. During prayer time worship to usher in the manifest presence of the Lord. Ushering in the manifest presence of the Lord is a necessity in deliverance ministry. When the glory of the Lord is present, you will experience supernatural and faster deliverances. As you praise Him together, your spirits are lifted and encouraged for the day and the enemy is hearing who you serve and adore! It puts the focus on God and not the devil. Play music at all times because God uses music in deliverance. A song might minister to someone and break open some inner healing. In a warfare song the demons can be expelled. It can be a song that has ministered to the person in the past and God will use it again. Stay in tune to the Holy Spirit and put in the music He is leading you to. God is always faithful to give you what you need. In the beginning of the session you might ask the client "What is your favorite music or what music do you like to listen to that ministers to you?" You could start with that music to ease their anxiety.

ITEMS NEEDED

Basic supplies to have on hand for your ministry sessions:

Tissue and trash - To be placed next to and pointed out to the client. It is amazing to see how many people simply overlook a tissue box.

Drinks - Water bottles, vitamin water or juice for your team members.

Mints - Fasting creates bad breath please be conscious of this. You don't want people you are praying over to be distracted by bad breath.

NOTEPADS AND PENS

Write notes on each client as the session is taking place. Write down what you have cast out and what you still have to work on and put it with their paperwork file for any follow up visits.

- Write down scriptures you are giving the client so they can take them home and meditate on them. Write down any book recommendations or things they need to work on or pray through.
- Instruct the team to write notes of discernment to each other and the leader.

REFERENCE BOOKS, MATERIALS AND LISTS

Do your deliverance in a room that has all your deliverance books in it so you are not running elsewhere should you need to refer to a book.

Use the books only as the Holy Spirit leads. He will always be faithful to direct you to the exact book and section He knows you need to assist the person in their freedom.

TOOLS OF WARFARE

Our ministry has items we use when in our deliverance sessions. They are not meant to be ritualistic or legalistic but simply anointed tools we choose to use in deliverance session as the Holy Spirit leads.

- WORSHIP OR PRAYER FLAGS – Flags consist of different colors which represent different spiritual meanings. The flags are waved by intercessors as the Holy Spirit leads during the session. They are used to usher in the presence of the Lord through worship at the beginning of a session. Flags like this should be smaller in size (2' x 3') to accommodate a standard room.

- PRAYER SHAWLS – All of our team members have at least one prayer shawl and wear them as the Holy Spirit leads. The Holy Spirit will direct us to the color or style to wear and whether or not to put one on the client while we are praying for them. Prayer shawls are comforting and we have had many testimonies that men and women hear more clearly from the Lord, their discernment increases and the distractions decrease.

- SHOFAR - The call of victory and deliverance. Many demons are expelled just at the sound of this rams horn.

"And seven priests shall bear seven trumpets of ram's horns before the ark. But the seventh day you shall march around the city seven times, and the priests shall blow the trumpets. It shall come to pass, when they make a long blast with the ram's horn, and when you hear the sound of the trumpet, that all the people shall shout with a great shout; then the wall of the city will fall down flat. And the people shall go up every man straight before him." Then Joshua the son of Nun called the priests and said to them, "Take up the Ark of the Covenant, and let seven priests bear seven trumpets of ram's horns before the ark of the LORD." –Josh. 6:4-6

- PRAYER STICKS – A prayer stick looks like a walking stick used as a tool in warfare, for prayer, worship and deliverance. Used as the Holy Spirit leads, He might call you to put them on the floor around people or touch a part of their body with them or to circle them in worship with the stick. Use caution when purchasing a prayer stick especially if you are purchasing it from a place that sells them as walking sticks. Look at the design and carefully pray while in the store if that is the stick the Lord wants you to have.
- ANOINTING OIL – Anoint the person you are ministering to as well as your team at the beginning of a session and use again during the session as led by the Spirit.

"And you shall take the anointing oil, pour it on his head, and anoint him." -Exodus 29:7

"Is anyone among you sick? Let him call for the elders of the church, and let them pray over him, anointing him with oil in the name of the Lord." -James 5:14

- MANTLES – These are narrower than a prayer shawl. We wear them when ministering, teaching at a deliverance school and also use them to impart ministry into people. When the session is complete we pray over the person and the Lord may give us a prophetic word for them or an instruction to pray over them an impartation for ministry. During this time we prayerfully consider which mantel the Lord would want them to have and place it on them during prayer.

BUILDING TRUST

It is important to start your sessions by building trust with your client. People that come into our ministry have been sent by referral. In our ministry there are a couple of different ways in which we build trust. The first recommendation we make before scheduling a deliverance session is that they attend one of our weekly or bi-weekly meetings. It gives them a chance to see how we operate, what we believe in and to get comfortable with us before their session. They will be able to discern us and see that serving the Lord is our heart's desire.

If they choose to attend one of your meetings use that opportunity to discern them. By being with them for a short period of time you can discern more what they are dealing with, how much time a session might take and if you are the deliverance ministry to assist them in their freedom. Sometimes you are not the ministry to help them and it can save them from feeling rejected if you can discern this early on.

Use this opportunity to explain in advance what deliverance ministry is. Not everyone coming for deliverance believes in deliverance or knows what deliverance is, especially if you have not personally talked to them. When someone is sent for a referral, often they will not know what they are getting into except that they were told by their friend "It was an awesome experience and you've got to do it." By talking with them ahead of time you can make sure they understand what will happen to them and how you are going to pray for them.

Another reason we encourage people to come to our meetings in advance is that sometimes people are delivered instantly in our meetings. This is absolutely incredible, so joyful and freeing. We love it when the glory of the Lord comes in and delivers in 5 minutes. This allows us to reach more people who need personal sessions. We find most people who are instantly delivered are ready and willing. They are eager to get the junk out of their trunk and many times do not have the need for follow up inner healing sessions. They usually don't have a lot of hurts and pains that they have to deal with or they have already dealt with the hurt and pain and just need the spirits that were attached to them kicked out.

When they attend our meetings, I make sure I tell one of my assistants I think they might be coming and to please make sure I get to meet them by the end of the day. This will show them you genuinely care about them and have an interest in setting them free. They will feel you were obtainable and reachable and not "too busy." Show people that you care, show them the same love Jesus would show them.

WORSHIP

Along with prayer, we believe worship stirs up the atmosphere in which we minister. Our intercessors and ministry is passionate about worship. People can be set free, healed and delivered just by worshiping our Lord. We were created to worship Him. I remember a time when I was in a worship service and praising my God I looked up at the screen and in the spiritual realm I saw the word "HEALED." I don't know what I was healed from that day, but I do know that my worship released a healing anointing upon my body and like the scripture says:

"But He was wounded for our transgressions, He was bruised for our iniquities; the chastisement for our peace was upon Him, and by His stripes we are healed." -Isaiah 53:5

"Who Himself bore our sins in His own body on the tree, that we, having died to sins, might live for righteousness—by whose stripes you were healed." -1 Peter 2:24

During your sessions, as the Holy Spirit leads, stop and worship the Lord. Worship increases the presence of the Lord, glorifies God and gives Him praise for what He is doing and gets your mind focused on the things above. It also refreshes and equips you to better minister to a person. Worship stirs up the atmosphere. Praise and worship changes the atmosphere. You want an atmosphere of praise in your sessions.

COMMUNICATION

Communication is the key. Encourage your client to communicate what they are feeling, thinking and hearing. I will tell them to please let me know if you get any thoughts in your head like this isn't working, I'm bored, or any other thoughts that come to your mind. I encourage and thank them often for their honesty and willingness to cooperate. By thanking them for their honesty it will not allow condemnation or judgment to come into them during the session. I advise them to let me know if they start feeling a pain in their body. If they start feeling a pain in their body that they did not walk in the session with, usually there is a demon attacking this part of the body. It is a distraction or a discernment that is where the demon is hiding and it is getting uncomfortable for them to be in there and they are starting to manifest. I will lay my hands on that part of their body and command it to go in Jesus' name. You need to be cautious and discern what they communicate with you. You can use it as a valuable tool to know what they are thinking and feeling. It can also be a distraction from the enemy to get you off track from what you really need to be doing. Take everything you receive to the Lord.

BATHROOM BREAKS

For your team members always leave two people with the client in the room at all times. Most of our sessions consist of three team members, therefore, if someone has to dismiss themselves to the restroom or for an emergency phone call there are still two people in the room.

For the client be aware of the amount of time they are spending in the bathroom. Keep an eye on them and check on them and ask them if they are alright if they linger for a long period of time. Make sure before dismissing them to use the restroom that they are conscious of where they are and what they are doing. If you are unsure, ask them to tell you your name and I ask them who is your Lord and Savior. You want to make sure the person is fully aware of their surroundings.

DISCERNMENT

During the session these are some routine things that can happen therefore be alert for any of the following:

- Is there a change in the atmosphere? Did you feel peace and now heaviness? We want to feel the presence of the Lord in our sessions. We have our discernment radar in high gear in our sessions and if we feel something amiss in the atmosphere we stop and discern what has happened, pray and worship if necessary.

- Watch the person's arms and hands and keep your eyes open at all times during deliverance, even while praying. If the person tries to touch you, gently and firmly say as not to startle them "You will not touch me in Jesus' name."

67

- Do not talk to a demon. If they try to talk, beg, distract and sidetrack you don't talk back to them. If they ask you a question, don't answer back. Don't ask the demons for information; we have the Holy Spirit to ask for information. Just simply ignore what they are saying, or say "Don't talk to me" and continue to cast it out.

- Distractions - If you start on one spirit and the person says "What about this or that" go back to the one you started on. Often a demon inside can be trying to confuse you and get you to leave that spirit alone and take you down a different trail. If the person is a mature Christian they can also help you deliver them during a session by feeding you information. Discern it and act on it if appropriate.

- Look deep into the person's eyes to see the demon. Look beyond the person into the demon so they can see the authority and Lordship of Jesus Christ in you.

- Manifestations – Look at people when they are starting to manifest. If you see a twitch in their body, their hand, head, foot or shoulder moves slightly, look at what demon names you were calling out when they started to move. If you are calling out multiple names and they are manifesting, pay close attention to the ones they are manifesting on and make sure you stay on the demon name or group of names until the twitching or movement stops. The demons are manifesting out of these locations and it will assist you in your discernment when those demons are gone.

- Facial expression – Watch their facial expressions, it will often tell you what is going on with a person. Pay attention to see if the demon is coming out or going back down inside them. Often they can feel a lump in their throat or tightness in their chest. This is usually the evil spirit moving. Take your authority and get it out. Ask them if they feel the release or if they feel peace. Don't be deceived that they always come out. Sometimes they are almost out and a person might get fear, doubt, unbelief, unworthiness or they can't forgive themselves for something and they will end up not being released of the demon. Make sure they feel a release and you have peace before you continue on to the next one.

- Trance – In some deliverance sessions the enemy will try to take the person into a trance. It can appear like they have been "slain in the spirit." The person's head can bob in different directions and they can appear sleepy and tired. If you get the discernment the demons are trying to take the person into a trance, simply say "In Jesus' name you will not take them into a trance." If you think they already went into a trance, get the person back, call out their name. Keep saying it until they make eye contact with you. Again ask them their name, your name, and who is their Lord and Savior.

- Drinks – If your client is thirsty allow them to have a drink of water. We suggest using a plastic cup or water bottle. We make sure the person is aware of their surroundings and if in doubt we will gently say "I command you not to spit water, throw the water or to gag or choke the person."

Be assured if the Lord is calling you into deliverance ministry He will give you what you need for each individual session. We can learn through observing and training by others. To learn more about doing a personal session please contact our ministry to host a deliverance school in your area.

CHAPTER 9

ROADBLOCKS

There are roadblocks we have occasionally encountered when delivering people of evil spirits. In order to minimize the number of roadblocks we may encounter, I periodically check in with our client to see how they are doing. Instead of just rolling forward with what we always think we should do, we need to stop and be sensitive to how the person we are ministering to is doing. Even though we operate in the gift of discernment there can be times we miss something. Stopping to check in with the client to communicate will help us be proactive in problem solving.

When I check in with a client I will ask them any of the following:

- Are you bored?
- Are you tired?
- Do you want to continue?
- Is this beneficial to you?
- Are you in physical pain anywhere?
- Do you feel anything moving or going on in your stomach?
- What are you feeling?
- Are you hearing any thoughts?
- Are you receiving this?

I encourage them to communicate honestly with me about what they are feeling. I assure them there are no wrong or right answers. I will even mention things I don't want them to be feeling so if they are a repeat client they don't get used to routine questions and answers. By asking these questions someone without a great gift of discernment can gain some valuable information. I proceed by binding in the spiritual realm what they are feeling. For example I might say "spirit of boredom, lying and complacency I bind you in Jesus' name. Mind binding, confusion and deaf and dumb spirits I command you not to activate and get out in Jesus' name." Take authority over what they are feeling so you can continue ministering effectively.

Just because they are feeling some of these manifestations it does not always mean they are under a demonic attack. Some of these are also signs of the glory of the Lord. We are looking for manifestations that do not feel good and are a distraction. Discern the information they give you and check your spirit to determine what kind of manifestation it is.

In approaching our client and asking for these insights we are talking to the client and not the demon. Remember we do not seek counsel or guidance from the demons. We are simply asking the person a few basic questions in order to increase our discernment, help us know the direction to head next and what more specifically to pray through. There are times when first starting out that your discernment isn't as strong or is blocked; it is times like these we can speak with our client and look for the direction we should move.

If it appears they are starting to not feel well I will ask them "Do you have a headache or is your stomach upset?" Remember we can feel in our bodies what they are feeling in theirs. So if you start feeling a pain in your leg while ministering ask them if they have a pain in their leg. After I confirm they are not feeling well, I will then pray healing over the area, command a spirit of affliction and infirmity to leave, and come against any spirits of frustration and distraction in Jesus' name. Your ministry time will not be effective if people are more focused on their physical feelings than on the words you are speaking into their lives.

BODY MOVEMENTS

I ask about body movements. I ask is your stomach upset or does it feel like it is rolling like a roller coaster? A lot of demonic movement takes place in the stomach and by finding out what is happening inside you can get a better grasp on the outside spiritual discernment. I bind upset stomachs, nausea and vomiting in Jesus' name. I could also ask, is there any movement in your body, any tingling, pain, distractions, heat or cold. This will help you to discern if they are undergoing a demonic attack while you are ministering to them.

MISCONCEPTIONS ABOUT DELIVERANCE

A roadblock to them not receiving would also be misconceptions about deliverance. In those cases I would ask why they are so scared. What are you afraid of? Explain to them how the session will go, that no response from them is necessary, that it is not based on their action or reactions, that the Lord is in charge and will do it. Try to ease what may be going through their mind.

NOT RECEIVING

People come in with such condemnation, bondage, distrust, fear, religion and tradition that they couldn't receive if they wanted to. The evil spirits have totally bound these persons and the person doesn't even know how to begin to let go of these issues. In these cases we pray against the above spirits and also pray off blocking, hindering spirits, mind binding and lying spirits. We don't just give up. Defeat is not an option!!! We want to try to assist the person to overcome what is blocking them from receiving everything the Lord has for them.

UNFORGIVENESS

If a person is not receiving then we will go back and check if there is any unforgiveness or sin in their life. We will make sure they have forgiven themselves and anyone in their life. We will explain that forgiveness is not a feeling it is a conscious decision to wipe the slate clean and to forgive the offender of the offense. It is not saying what happened was okay. It is saying Jesus purchased our forgiveness at the cross and today, even though we don't "feel" like it in our heart, we are making a conscious decision to forgive the person who has offended us and wipe the slate clean so we aren't held in bondage anymore. We explain most of the time the person doesn't even know we are hurt by their actions. We are holding ourselves in bondage to the offense and unforgiveness by not letting it go. We simply ask them to release it to Jesus because, in our heads, we know it is the right thing to do and then we ask Jesus to put our heart in alignment with the forgiveness in His timing.

NO JUDGMENT

We tell a client there is nothing that you can say that will make us judge you or that most likely we haven't heard before. We couldn't do what we do if we judged people. God has not given us a spirit of judgment. I actually ask the Lord when I am done with the session to erase what I have learned so if I ever see the person on the street I will not remember their junk.

Unfortunately, the people do continue to surprise us. Just when we think we have heard it all or seen it all, we experience something else shocking. Most of it we are able to digest and not act shocked. However, I do remember one occasion where we were in a session and something new came up. I want to share this experience for the health of you and your team on how to handle such experiences. We had been ministering to this person for about 2 hours when she revealed something that set us all back. Of course, being women, this attacked the very core of our being. No one could have imagined something so horrific happening to a person and it set us all back. We were all stunned, shocked, floored and overwhelmed with emotion of what this person was forced to go through.

I encourage you to keep your composure. Don't let them think or know you are shocked, we didn't. Act the same and keep it inside like it didn't make a difference. Don't wear your feelings or emotions on your face, you don't want to add to the situation. The team showed no emotion, no tears on their face but in the spirit realm I could tell they were devastated. I decided for the sake of the team to end the session for that day. As I had the opportunity, I simply told the client we had gone far enough for one day, prayed over her, filled her with the Holy Spirit and sent her on her way.

Afterward, the team and I sat for a while and talked about what just happened. We put music on and just soaked in the presence of the Lord. I couldn't let them leave with heaviness or feeling burdened. We took the opportunity to learn from it and move forward. Your team is your most important asset and you need to take care of your team. Never jeopardize your team emotionally, physically or spiritually. Treat them as your family because they are your spiritual family, and you need them as much as they need you.

PRAYER

If there is blockage and we are getting nowhere, I will often go back to prayer. As my team members give the client a break or just talk socially with them for a few minutes, I will lie prostrate and pray and ask the Lord for direction. I will humble myself right there in the room with the client and go on my face in prayer to the Father above for direction and discernment.

CHANGE DIRECTIONS

Inner healing and deliverance go hand in hand. It can be a matter of where do you start first with inner healing or deliverance. We think we need to go in one direction when we need to go in another. You cannot walk a person through inner healing without deliverance and you cannot walk a person through deliverance without inner healing. Therefore, if you are off in one direction and blocked try the other.

APPLICATION

Revisit your application. On one occasion I was getting frustrated and we couldn't get total freedom for the person. I had tried everything and I went to prayer. After coming out of prayer I had the discernment to look at their application again. I had noticed they had circled that their uncle had been into freemasonry. This persons spouse was upstairs and I went to talk to them. I had discovered that the person and uncle had a very close relationship (soul tie). I discovered the uncle probably dedicated the client to the masons. I went back downstairs into the session and started casting off these spirits and the person was set free.

DEMONIC MANIFESTATION

If someone starts staring at you a demon has possibly taken over. In this case you have what we call "lost the person." The person you are ministering to has gone "down under." They aren't hearing what you are speaking to them and the demon is at the front of them and you are speaking to the demon. Stop your ministry session and get the person back. Say "(person's name) are you with me?" and get the person to acknowledge you. You will kind of see them snap out of it. Their face will change and their eyes will soften, kind of like taking them out of a daze or day dream. Ask them "(person's name) do you know my name, do you know where you are?" Talk to them for a few minutes and then ask them if they are okay to continue.

PHYSICAL DISTRACTIONS

Physical distractions can sometimes throw a session off and create outside disruption where you are not able to keep the flow of the Spirit going. This could include lawn mowers or snow blowers from outside, stereos skipping, someone knocking at your door, someone cleaning your ministry center and other things. Be aware and conscious of these in advance. Close your windows, schedule appointments when maintenance people are not working, etc.

FRUSTRATION

Frustration can set in when your client doesn't remember. Take into consideration many people are stuffers and stuff their feelings and emotions rather than deal with them. When this happens, we have to lean on the Holy Spirit's timing to release to them the information He wants them to have. There are a couple of different case scenarios here. Sometimes people have purposely forgotten what has happened to them because it is too painful to deal with or they don't want to face reality. Other people have been taught to bury their problems, that no one needs to know what happened to them and to pretend everything on the outside is fine.

People have a natural tendency to not remember what happened because they were too young. They might feel that something is not quite right or they might suspect that something has happened but, for the majority, they have absolutely no idea they have been defiled, abused, or other things that have happened to them. In this case, the Lord will reveal the issues in His timing. Don't try to bring something out without proper timing and affirmation from the Lord.

During our sessions, the Lord can reveal to us pieces of information such as the person has been sexually abused or they had a forced abortion. The person doesn't remember these things happening to them because they were so traumatic, they stuffed them or chose to forget them. We have found that sometimes the Lord gives us this information in order to effectively minister to the person about another issue. It is relative, He reveals it to us, but it is not time to reveal it to the client.

The client can feel frustrated because they can't believe what has been revealed by the Holy Spirit. This is not meant to be an obstacle but meant for them to have the spirits cast off. God wants to set us free and part of supernatural deliverance is that we don't have to know about it or analyze it; we need to just let Him set us free from it. Be cautious when ministering that the client doesn't get caught up in what has been revealed in the spirit. People have a tendency to have analytical minds and, in these cases, they need to shut down the processing and just let God have control.

When your client is frustrated, minister to their immediate needs. Meet them where they are at with compassion and love. If you have been through a similar experience, share your testimony with them so they know they are not alone. Be careful, I like to prelude my testimony with "Even though I don't know exactly what you are going through or how you feel because all situations are truly different, I want to tell you about a time I had a similar experience." Remember, even if you had a miscarriage and they had a miscarriage how two people handle that can be totally different. For example, I had a miscarriage and even though

I suffered a loss and grief and would love for my child to be alive today, I was alright. My friend suffered a miscarriage and had to meet with a counselor for a period of time to get emotional assistance to handle her loss. Your parents could have died and their parent could have died and even though you both experienced the death of a parent, what you exactly felt and how you exactly handled that was different and we need to acknowledge that as such. Don't pretend to know 100% exactly what they went through or are going through.

Frustration can also happen if a client isn't following our direction or following the prompting of the Holy Spirit. In circumstances when the client isn't cooperating, it is best to end the session. If they are wasting your time, not being completely honest, going in different directions and causing confusion and stress, then it is best to end the session. "For where envy and self-seeking exist, confusion and every evil thing are there" (James 3:16). You don't have a client who is cooperative enough to continue and you need to end the session.

Frustration can set in because they aren't persistent enough to press in and conquer what you have advised them to overcome. This can include a behavior pattern, habit or addiction. These people need inner healing and good Christian people to walk along side them, helping them to overcome their strongholds. Many times while you are consistently ministering to someone you are going to have to help them along. This can come by establishing them into a group of spirit filled believers who will walk beside them, help them grow, teach, equip, train and mentor them. Assigning them or encouraging them to find an accountability partner or mentor who they can be held accountable to for their actions and who they can confess to when they slip up. We recommend people to attend our weekly meetings where they can get further training, equipping and prayer. We also give them what we call "homework" between sessions. We find what they are struggling with, having difficulty conquering or what the Holy Spirit wants them to work on. We pick one or two things that they can handle growing in or trying to give up and we encourage them to just focus on these one or two things until the next time we meet. We try to give them a smaller more obtainable goal than trying to hit them with changing everything at once.

TEAM FRUSTRATION

There was one case that took us longer than any other. It was intense and a long session. I hate to admit it but we were getting worn down. So what did I do? What I do every other time I need the Lord, get face down. I stopped the session got face down in prayer, sought the Lord and came out of the time with some holy righteous anger and the discernment I needed to get the client free. A double bonus and God got all the glory.

ROADBLOCK ASSISTANCE

Look in your reference books. If I get discernment to look in a book I will often find the answer.

I recommend these books for spirit listing and assistance; *Spiritual Warfare* by Richard Ing, *So Free* by William Sudduth and *Delivering the Captives* by Alice Smith.

CALL FOR ASSISTANCE

Call or text someone more experienced and ask for their advice while you are with the client.

CALL IN THE PROFESSIONALS

Call in people more spiritually mature, more experienced in the subject or that specialize in certain areas of deliverance. Even though I have a lot of experience, I used to have a person I called in on my hard core witchcraft cases. She isn't more experienced or confident in deliverance but she was just as knowledgeable in the witchcraft area and sometimes two heads are better than one. Don't be concerned about losing your client to another ministry by referring them to a deliverance ministry or someone other than yourself. We are not in competition with each other.

END THE SESSION

The person has been this way a long time and leaving them like this a few more days or weeks isn't going to hurt them. Perhaps it isn't their timing. Take it back to prayer and fasting to get the direction you need.

DOUBT AND UNBELIEF

Is there any doubt and unbelief present in the room? If you feel there is doubt in the person or the people ministering, take authority over it. If it is in the person you are ministering to, command doubt and unbelief to leave in Jesus' name. If it is in a person on the team I would suggest removing them from the room for the remainder of your session. Jesus removed the doubt and unbelief out of the room and so should we.

TEAM OBSTACLE

Is anyone in the room on the team struggling with the same issue that you are hitting a roadblock against? Often, we have behavior patterns and habits to conquer as part of our deliverance. We have a tendency to sin from time to time and to allow our familiar demons or the things that have challenged us back in. In these cases, if a team member is struggling with the same issue or demon that the client is struggling with, the demons can start feeding off each other. It means that they can get stronger and give us more resistance coming out. In that case, we also recommend that you get your team member who is struggling out of the room. It is in the best interest of your client so they can be set free, for the team member so they don't get tormented or any ungodly attachments, defilements and transferences and for the remainder of the team so they can take complete authority over that demon, to get rid of it in Jesus' name.

To conquer the roadblocks in the future we suggest you practice discerning and develop your gifting. Go to a public place and pray and scan the crowd and see if any words of knowledge or prophetic insights come up in your spirit. Read further books on the deliverance and how to set people free and get involved in a ministry locally where you can observe and be mentored for deliverance ministry.

CHAPTER 10

HOW TO DO A DELIVERANCE SESSION

The following are details on how to do a deliverance session. Even though these are guidelines, I encourage you to have a team of intercessors and a release from the Holy Spirit that He wants you to enter deliverance ministry and start doing sessions. The guidelines I give you are practical applications based on knowledge as you grow in your discernment with the Lord. These instructions are basic so that you could lead a session based off a form and the guidelines executed here.

As your client approaches, have one of your assistants ready to greet them at the door. The client will be nervous, a friendly welcoming face at the door may ease their nerves. I recommend having a team member and not the founder or leader welcome them at the door. A greeting by a team member is less intimidating to the client than meeting the founder or leader of their session right away.

Have the team make casual conversation to lighten their fears and burdens and then the leader of the session walks in and introduces themself. Try to relax the person you are ministering to by asking them casual questions relating to the deliverance session. Do not get off track by asking about their family or the weather. You need to keep focused and not give any room for a spirit of distraction to begin to attack. Ask them if they had nightmares the night before and if they say yes, encourage them by saying that it is normal. They might tell you satan gave them car trouble, their stomach is nauseated or the enemy didn't want them to make it here. Again, light heartedly say "Yes that's normal but we will take care of it." If they haven't already exposed it, ask if they are nervous and again they usually will respond with yes. Tell them it's normal, try and relax and pray some peace into them. Make them as comfortable as you can with what is about to happen.

STARTING A SESSION HOUSEKEEPING RULES

After the leader has helped them relax a little we then proceed. It is important to get them to relax a little before you begin the housekeeping rules, otherwise they may not even hear what you are trying to tell them.

Before we start the session, we have one of our assistants go over the following with the client to get them comfortable with us and give them a little information with what is going to happen. Our team member might even read this from a sheet of paper to make sure they don't forget anything. We tell them:

- We will be communicating with each other by writing things down and also may whisper to each other. We are confirming with each other to make sure we are doing what the Holy Spirit is leading us to do and that we are in agreement. (People need to know this in advance or it can feed a spirit of rejection and make them distracted.)

- We ask you to please not pray and just receive during this time whatever the Lord has for you.

- We will be praying in English and in tongues, tongues is our way of communicating with God and allowing God to flow in us and through us. It helps us to get more direction from God. (If they are not familiar with praying in tongues we explain it to them. If they have never heard tongues I will even say "Tongues sound like this" and I will pray aloud in tongues in front of them for a sentence. By praying aloud in tongues in front of them I have taken away the "shock and awe" factor of when it does happen and have minimized distractions.)

- Do you currently have any pain on your body? (We pray healing and ask God to release it so that it is not a distraction in the session. It lets us know what they have walked in with so that we know if there are any additional attacks or concerns during the session.)

- Inform us if you get nauseated or start feeling angry like you want to hit us. We have complete authority over all these things and they have never happened in our sessions but please let us know if you start feeling that way.

- You may or may not feel anything. (Some people are performance driven and think they have to feel something is happening. If they don't, they get discouraged and doubt sets in. We let them know early on that they may or may not feel anything happening.)

- Let us know if you are having thoughts such as; nothing is happening, they are lying to me, I'm bored, have doubt and unbelief, or are being distracted etc. (Encourage them to communicate with you, be careful to discern the information they give you if it is from the person and not a demon trying to cause distraction.)

- We will be putting our hands on different parts of your body depending on how the Holy Spirit leads, let us know if it makes you uncomfortable at any time. We usually touch your head, shoulder or stomach.

- One of us may ask you to repeat something after us, usually a prayer of renunciation or a prayer to forgive someone. If you don't agree with what we are asking you to repeat just skip it. (We generally make sure they have all their unforgiveness and renunciation done ahead of time. We want to get to the hard issues with them, the items they can't handle on their own. Therefore, we only do renunciation and unforgiveness when we are encountering a roadblock, legal right or stronghold.)

- Do you have any questions? (Choose carefully which and how to answer.)

- Please try not to analyze but just receive what the Lord has for you.
- Can you tell me when you made Jesus your Lord and Savior? (Make sure they are saved.)
- We make sure they are aware that this is a session to expel evil spirits or demons and make sure they have an understanding and acknowledge these can be in them as a Christian.

Anoint the client with oil and pray for peace and understanding to come upon them. Anointing oil can be found at most Christian bookstores or you can use blessed olive oil from your kitchen cupboard. Put a little on your finger and make the shape of the cross on their forehead in order to anoint them.

At the beginning of the session you want to bind some spirits from activating in advance. Speak out loud and command there will be no violence, headaches, upset stomachs, vomiting and anger. Simply say "I bind anger, headaches, upset stomachs, vomiting and violence in Jesus' name."

Pray and ask the Holy Spirit to convict them and bring anything into remembrance that He wants them or us to know about. Make sure they have forgiven themselves and anyone else for anything before you start the session. Explain to them forgiveness is not a feeling but a conscious decision to accept the atoning work of the cross and release the person from the debt you feel they owe you through the act they committed against you. Tell them you don't have to "feel" like forgiving, however that you are making a conscious choice that it is the right thing to do in order to move on. If they are having a difficult time forgiving, explain forgiveness to them more in depth and lead them through forgiving the people in their life. Encourage them to speak aloud, "I forgive (person's name) for (person's act)" or "I forgive (person's name)". Afterward, you need to make sure they have forgiven themselves. Instruct them to speak out "I forgive myself." It is very difficult for most people to forgive themselves and you might have to have them repeat it several times. Watch the expression on their face as they repeat it. Watch for the tears to flow or the reality of the forgiveness to sink in.

Start by casting out spirits of doubt and unbelief, distraction, and lying and deceitful spirits. You might have to do this a few times during the session. You may receive further discernment from the Lord during the session that these spirits are trying to attack again. If someone has been bound in religion, I suggest you cast off all the religious spirits so that you can proceed without interruption. The religious spirits would include; religion, tradition, denominationalism and legalism.

Review their application and continue by asking them, "What is the biggest thing holding you back from receiving the fullness of God?" Many times this question alone will give you insight into their situation and will expose their strongman. Bind or cast out their strongman depending on the discernment you are getting from the Holy Spirit. There are variances in the way people deal with the strongman. We have found from experience sometimes he is the first and sometimes he is the last to go out. Either way, do the biblical instruction and bind the strongman. "Or how can one enter a strong man's house and plunder his goods, unless he first binds the strong man? And then he will plunder his house" (Matt 12:29).

There is a difference between binding and casting out. Binding is simply taking authority and saying you are not going to activate in this session. Casting out is taking it out, sometimes we take it out early on and sometimes at the end. Listen to the Holy Spirit's direction, He will lead and guide you. Either way, speak out "Strongman of (The person's strongman spirit name based on what they told you was the biggest thing holding them back from receiving the fullness of God.) I bind you in the name of Jesus Christ."

We will then proceed with any discernment we are getting from the Lord of spirits that could be attached or work together with the strongman. This is where, for those of you who aren't operating in the gift of discernment yet, could use your knowledge. For example, if someone has a spirit of lust, they could have spirits of masturbation, pornography, sexual abuse and other sexual spirits. Using common sense, think about what spirits would attach to lust. This is how you can operate in a session without the gift of discernment. If someone has stress, they could have anxiety, fear and worry. Think about what in the natural would go with what is happening in the spiritual.

87

You could purchase books that list the spirit names which would assist you in knowing what spirits are grouped together. Two great books to purchase would be *The Demon Hit List* by John Eckhardt or *The Rules of Engagement Vol. 2* by Dr. N. Cindy Trimm. These books have detailed listings of what spirits belong together and can be used as a guide as you grow in your discernment.

We operate in a strong gift of discernment, therefore, we are going to wait for the Holy Spirit to lead us in the direction He wants us to go. It would be very easy for us to function in the knowledge of what we know and what makes sense but we want to be led by the Spirit of God and do what He wants. We need to put ourselves and our experiences aside and let the Holy Spirit lead the session because every session is different. We are quiet and wait for His direction and discernment. We do nothing without His permission to go ahead and start. Please do not be uncomfortable with silence and waiting for the presence of the Lord to come. There have been times when we will be quiet and just go over to the person and evil spirits will start flying out. We will just walk over, and the glory of the Lord will be present and demons will start expelling without us even calling them out by name. All we need is the power of God to fall. Glory to God!

I realize not everyone is operating in the gift of discernment and while you are waiting for that gift to develop, please use the knowledge you have. If you start operating in the Spirit and then get stuck, go to your application. That is why an application is helpful. We have included a sample application in the back of this book for your reference.

To do deliverance according to the application, there are a couple of different methods you can use. I would suggest quickly reviewing the application to yourself and see if the Lord leads you to a particular area. Is there something that is sticking out, or that you keep going back to? Start where you felt you were quickened to. After you are done with the part that you were led to, you can review and pray over the application again to see if the Lord wants you to go to a particular area again. Keep doing this until the application is finished or you are blocked and can't get any further direction. When you can't get any further direction you then need to pray and discern if the Lord is calling you to quit for the day, or if you need to start at the beginning of the application and go over anything you didn't already cover.

If you didn't feel the Lord call you to a particular area of the application, start going one question at a time and talk to them about it, make sure they have had inner healing in that area, or are at peace with what happened. Ask them if they have dealt with the item and if they are ready to move forward. I would then cast out the spirit that is associated with the question. As you cast the spirit out watch their facial expressions and wait for a release from the Lord that the spirit is gone.

When casting out demons always fill them back up with the opposite of what you cast out of them. After casting out a series of spirits fill them up again with the Holy Spirit. The Bible instructs us in Matthew 12:43-45 "When an unclean spirit goes out of a man, he goes through dry places, seeking rest, and finds none. Then he says, 'I will return to my house from which I came.' And when he comes, he finds it empty, swept, and put in order. Then he goes and takes with him seven other spirits more wicked than himself, and they enter and dwell there; and the last state of that man is worse than the first. So shall it also be with this wicked generation."

Pray and invite the Holy Spirit to come in and refill those spots. In addition, pray to fill them up with the opposite of what you just cast out. For example, if you cast out stress fill them up with peace, if you cast out rejection fill them up with acceptance and if you cast out hate fill them up with love. Discern what in the natural is the opposite of what you just cast out and pray to fill them up with that emotion.

Keep casting out and filling up until your questionnaire is complete or you feel a release from the Holy Spirit. You will get additional discernment as to when to end a session through the Ending a Session chapter of this book. When you are finished allow them to gather their composure before dismissing them from your ministry. Pray a prayer of peace and blessing over them before you end for the day.

CHAPTER 11

GENERATIONAL CURSES

"You shall not bow down to them nor serve them. For I, the LORD your God, am a jealous God, visiting the iniquity of the fathers upon the children to the third and fourth generations of those who hate Me, but showing mercy to thousands, to those who love Me and keep My commandments." -Exodus 20:5-6

"And the LORD passed before him and proclaimed, The LORD, the LORD God, merciful and gracious, longsuffering, and abounding in goodness and truth, keeping mercy for thousands, forgiving iniquity and transgression and sin, by no means clearing the guilty, visiting the iniquity of the fathers upon the children and the children's children to the third and the fourth generation." -Exodus 34:6-7

Educating yourself and discovering generational curses in our family lines are imperative to setting the captives free. I believe, as a body of believers, we have been too complacent in casting off and breaking generational curses. It is not as simple as we have thought it was for years. We cannot just lay hands on someone complacently or hastily and say "All generational curses be gone in Jesus' name" and expect them to leave. Yes in certain cases they do. You could compare it to why sometimes people receive a healing and sometimes they receive a miracle. We do not know why people receive instant deliverance and sometimes they take longer, but the fact is it happens just like in the cases of healings or miracles.

As a body of believers, we have been too complacent and not informed enough in the severity of generational curses. I have been around many spirit filled, tongue talking Christians who operate in a healing anointing, working and ministering in healing ministries, that are trying to take their authority over these curses and the people are not experiencing true freedom in Christ. How do I know? Because these are the very people that have been sent to my ministry. People who truly can't get free, whose demons are following them. People who are crying out to me how desperate they are to be free of how their parents created them to be or raised them. We ask people coming into our ministry if they have ever received deliverance prayer before, and over half of them say yes. When I ask about getting prayer for generational curses I find myself getting the same response. Yes, they were broken and then I proceed to ask if they are free. I ask if they are still fighting the same demons and they are, and not only them, but their children. It excites me so much when I can deliver both a father and mother and then they bring their children in for deliverance. Nothing brings me greater joy than to start a new family line of people free of generational curses and filled with blessings! Glory to God!

In order to break ourselves from the generational curses that plague us we first have to realize what generational curses are at work in our lives. For this I ask people to do a family tree. I ask them to go back to their grandparents or great grandparents, whoever they have knowledge of and write down the facts. I ask them to also list their siblings and their children on the tree. Under each person's name I have them list all their emotional and physical challenges and struggles. Under the person's name for emotional issues they would list items such as depression, bipolar, fear and other emotional imbalances. For physical challenges, I am looking for inherited medical diseases such as glaucoma, diabetes, high blood pressure and other physical ailments.

By listing out this family tree we can usually find the entry point. In certain circumstances, where we have a stronghold we are trying to break, we want to see who committed the sin that allowed these curses to enter and repent on their behalf. We can break these curses at the entry point so they don't affect the person we are ministering to.

We also find by listing the generational curses, where the strongholds are. An emotional response of bitterness is usually linked to cancer, fear can be related to asthma and allergies. If we can tag the emotional response and link it to the physical cause, it will give us more discernment into breaking the spiritual stronghold and generational curse.

We don't understand why some are healed instantly and some are healed as they go, I believe some curses go instantly and some of them, like our healing and deliverance, we have to go to the root of the problem. By researching our family tree we can get to the root of the problem.

We need to realize that a curse is at work in our lives. We need to study our past and discern what has come down through the generations and is affecting us today. Make a list of what is in your past. You are not claiming it is in your family or calling it forth. You are educating yourself in order for the Lord to work in your life. In order for Him to refine you and purify you. Make sure the items in your past are cut off, broken and not going to affect you, your family or those you love. Break things off such as divorce, alcohol, heart attacks, glaucoma, depression and control.

Worldly studies show and I rebuke this for you and cancel the curse in Jesus name.

- That a child who was sexually abused will often become a child abuser.
- Someone who is from a divorced family will often become divorced themselves.
- A person raised in an alcoholic home will often become an alcoholic.

I rebuke that for all of you according to Galatians 3:13 "Christ has redeemed us from the curse of the law, having become a curse for us" (for it is written, "cursed is everyone who hangs on a tree")." We have been redeemed from the curse!

We don't claim it or own that in our lives because we know:

- "All things are possible for God." -Mark 10:27.
- "And we know that all things work together for good to those who love God." -Romans 8:28.
- "We have victory through our Lord Jesus Christ." -1 Corinthians 15:57.

However, the world's statistics show you these things can follow us and reoccur. I want you to know today that you can be redeemed from these things, you can be different, you can be changed and you can be free! You are like who your parents created you to be but you can become like who your Heavenly Father created you to be, made in His image. Glory to God! It is time to take back what the enemy has stolen from us. It is time for us to take our rightful place and place of authority. Christ has taken this from us but we need to do our part and break it off our lives so we can live in victory.

How do you break the curses off? By calling them out individually by name. Speak aloud, "I break off or cast out a generational curse of divorce in Jesus' name or, generational curse of depression go in Jesus' name." Whatever you are dealing with, call it out by name with the word generational curse before it if you have determined it is a generational curse. If you see a lot of a particular spirit through the generations, I would pray strongman generational curse of that particular spirit go in Jesus' name. I am going to call everything out by name and wait for the Holy Spirit to give me a release on each spirit. I want to make sure they are gone.

I lived in bondage to a generational spirit of fear for 40 years. Fear would grip me because it was a curse in my family line. All the women and probably some of the men had fear. Issues would arise in my life and I could feel the curse of fear just pierce my insides. I can now say I have been completely set free and delivered from this spirit of fear. My spirit is having a party right now just thinking about it. Glory to God! It took me over two years to be delivered of this spirit of fear. I had to continually seek the Lord for direction and discernment into this family curse, what the entry point was and why I was still allowing it to grip me.

I had to overcome my thought patterns, behaviors patterns, and where my mind naturally wanted to go. I had to "no longer conform to this world (of fear) but be transformed by the renewing of my mind" (Romans 12:2). That is what I did. I cried out to God all the time to renew my mind. I had my friend pray over me for my mind to be renewed. I had to take authority over this fear and my thoughts. I needed to be free from this fear and you can be too! Glory to God!

People of God whatever your stronghold, whatever your curse you can be free, you will be free, just believe! In John 8:36 it says "Therefore if the Son makes you free, you shall be free indeed." Jesus came to set the captives free and He said in John 10:10 "I have come that they may have life, and that they may have it more abundantly." Living in fear, living in generational curses is not abundant living. That is why our ministry is different. We aren't going to settle for anything less than complete freedom, than the abundant living He has promised us!

We have generational curses we don't even realize. I know someone who would say "I have a love hate relationship with my sister. Half the time we love each other and half of the time it is a challenge being around her." The words she was speaking were not helping in her relationship with her sister. In fact, I realized this was a generational curse in her life. Both of her parents had that kind of relationship with their siblings. She would remember as a child her parents verbally fighting with their siblings and the years of silence they would go through. However, I felt I needed to break the curses off her and her children. The Bible says in Matt. 10:35-36 "For I have come to 'set a man against his father, a daughter against her mother, and a daughter-in-law against her mother-in-law'; and 'a man's enemies will be those of his own household." However, it also says in Heb. 12:14 "Pursue peace with all people, and holiness, without which no one will see the Lord." She also knew she had to change her word choices to further break the curse.

Here are some word choices you may want to think about in order to avoid and prevent any new generational curses from rising up.

- "That makes me sick or you make me sick," when someone tells you something or shows you something can open a doorway to sickness and disease.

- "She's driving me crazy or I can't take it anymore" leads to emotional doors being opened for stress, panic anxiety and mental instability.
- "We can't afford that" – instead say "We are waiting for our financial blessing or we are choosing not to spend our money on that". Change your mentality so that you don't put a poverty mindset on your children.
- "Don't say to your children I am going to kill you for that" which can lead to a spirit of death.
- "You irritate me" can lead to a spirit of irritation.

We not only inherit physical traits but also emotional and spiritual traits. We need to make sure we are not curse starters. Think about all the words that were spoken over you, how you were treated, it makes you who you are today and we certainly don't want to do that to our children.

What about things spoken like:

- She can't read or she struggles in the language arts area
- She sings off key
- He always drops something
- He is lazy
- My kids are loud and obnoxious
- Her middle name is trouble maker

Don't curse your children and spouse with your words. If it doesn't edify, encourage or exhort don't say it. Don't take the chance of starting new generational curses. If you have said those things break those curses off your children and spouse. Right now say *"Heavenly Father, I repent and renounce every idle word, negative word, every word that did not edify, exhort, encourage and comfort another person. I break all word curses off my children right now in Jesus' name."*

For those of you who believe casting off generational curses can be simpler than this I ask you:

- Are you seeing it go?

- Are you seeing the manifestations of freedom in this person's life?
- Is there life producing fruit in this area?
- Are they being used to share their testimony in this area to help free other people?
- Are you seeing the healing and complete deliverance?
- Is there any follow up with the person to know the lasting effects?
- Are you seeing instant results of what occurred?
- Are you witnessing behavior patterns and habits changed?
- Are the people complaining about the same things over and over?
- Have they come back to you for ministry in the same area?

We need to arise and believe there is more to generational curses than complacency. We cannot simply lay our hands on people and say generational spirits be gone. It is so much deeper than that. I will continue more education and training in a future book I am writing on generational curses. However, while you are starting deliverance ministry, follow some of the simple guidelines I have given you and go a little deeper than you think you should and watch how the Lord will set His people free!

CHAPTER 12

ENDING A SESSION

When determining to end the session or when someone is clean I ask myself "Are we ever really clean or are we clean for that season of our life?" In Deut 7:22-23 it says "And the LORD your God will drive out those nations before you little by little; you will be unable to destroy them at once, lest the beasts of the field become too numerous for you. But the LORD your God will deliver them over to you, and will inflict defeat upon them until they are destroyed." Right here it states the land will be given little by little. We need to maintain this season of deliverance before we obtain another season of deliverance. We need to be faithful in what He has given us so that He can give us more. In 2 Cor 1:10 it reaffirms that deliverance is a process by saying "Who delivered us from so great a death, and does deliver us; in whom we trust that He will still deliver us."

I have learned through deliverance ministry that even if we think that person is clean, they are clean for that season or reason of their life. We have let people leave our care only to find out later they had more to deal with. Even in my own life and my husband's, I can tell you that there were times we thought we were clean only to go to another level. I explain it as the deeper you grow in Christ the more the Father wants to clean out. As you receive more and more of the Holy Spirit, He starts to push out all that isn't of God. We are not like Jesus until

He comes again. Therefore, we always have more to clean up and give up to God.

There are things in our conscious; things we know about that we have had to deal with such as our anger, hurts, disappointments, etc... But as the Holy Spirit continues to infill us and dwell within us, we are shown things from the Father that we weren't ready spiritually to handle before, such as sexual abuses, rejection as a teenager and things that subconsciously bother us that we can't quite put our finger on. We feel there is something not right, something that prevents us from receiving the fullness of God and still something we can't seem to let go of. We can't quite put our finger on it but know it is there. There are behavior patterns, attitudes or perhaps a lack of joy in our life that we can't seem to conquer to be able to live in victory. Often, it is because these things are attached to something greater that is still inside. There are times something happens in our life and it still brings up a hurt or irritant when we think about it, an offense that keeps rising up time after time. These are usually caused by a deeper hurt, a bigger root that we didn't even know we had.

Our Father loves us so much that over time He continues to work on us to get all our junk out and make us more like Him. I remember a time in my life when I was considering studying a specific topic and when I did, it revealed something that happened to me in my past that I didn't even know about. I remember questioning God as to why I had to know about something that was not currently afflicting me. I dealt with this issue for months and the Holy Spirit very gently guided me through it. After I completed the healing process I had a joy and freedom which could not even be described in words.

My mentor once asked me "If you had to go through it all over again and not know about what you discovered, would you?" I said, no way! The joy and freedom I now have was worth the hurt, pain and revelation I had to go through. It was like the chains were broken off and I was released from the gates of hell and I didn't even know I was bound. I was ministering, doing conferences, teaching, and delivering people weekly, all while there was still something in me that needed to be delivered.

We are not going to be like Christ until He comes again. There are always going to be things we need to work on, new levels we need to go to, but I believe the Lord also does it as we are able to handle it. We go through deliverance and the team gets the discernment we are clean and I believe we are clean for that season, until we are mature enough to handle more and until we have walked out that part of our life in victory. After we have walked in victory and have been refreshed and refilled, the Lord will come back and do another level or, like I often say, another layer. I like to refer to myself as an onion being peeled, layer upon layer at a time, of all the flesh, of all the sin, of all unrighteousness so I can be in righteous standing in Christ.

If we are a continual work in progress, how do you know if a person is clean for this season, for the day or when to end the prayer session. I believe when I get a clean or clear and our team discerns it that the person is clean. They can go out and walk in victory and continue daily living. We are constantly asking each other during a prayer session, do you have a clear on that one? Meaning is that spirit gone, did you see it or feel it leave? We want to know spirit by spirit or for a group of spirits instead of going back at the end and trying to figure out what might still be there. At the end, we take a couple of moments to pray and seek the Lord for further direction and discernment into what is happening in the spiritual realm. We want to make sure we haven't opened a bag of worms (demons) and leave that person manifesting or stirred up. We want to make sure our work is complete for that day. The Lord will communicate with us whether the person is done, needs follow up inner healing, has "homework" to do or needs another follow up prayer session. When scheduling follow up appointments we often give them an appointment card automatically, or the Lord will tell us to have them call us for a follow up visit.

Ending a session has come with years of experience, and although we do not face most of this now, I want to educate you as you are learning, equipping and growing in this ministry and your authority, what you can come up against. First of all, I recommend you read the book *Destined for Dominion*, which you can obtain through our ministry. It is one of the best books we have ever read on our authority in Christ. You need to know your authority in order to be able to cast out demons and overcome any challenges or obstacles. As you become comfortable with the demonic and know your authority, these challenges won't seem to overcome you.

HOMEWORK

There are sessions in which we determine the Lord wants to give our client homework. When they have been in bondage to rejection, people pleasing, smoking, pornography or lying spirits we want to permanently help them overcome these. These spirits can be a layering process because these spirits also result in behavior patterns, habits and addictions. We cast out the spirits of these bondages and then have them walk it out for a period of time. We advise them to go home and try to stop smoking, take authority over the lying spirits, don't take in the rejection, stop people pleasing, etc... We advise them that we believe the Lord will deliver them from more, after they walk out and conquer their current bondages by actively breaking the habits, addictions and behavior patterns. We tell them, even though the spirits have left you; you still have to overcome the habit of reaching for the cigarette to have something in your mouth, to not turn on the internet to watch pornography or not be a people pleaser by doing everything for everyone. When they feel they have made progress we invite them to call us for a follow up visit.

REJECTION

When ending a session early you have to be conscious that the client doesn't take on a spirit of rejection. The client can perceive it as turning them away, not being able to help them or that they are too messed up to become free. Be careful of those who have been in the bondage of rejection, they could experience ending a session prematurely as more rejection. If they are dealing with rejection I always recommend the book *Approval Addiction* by Joyce Meyer.

Let them know you care about them with the agape love the Bible speaks about. Tell them you are not leaving them, you are not giving up on them and neither is God. Simply advise them that God occasionally gives us homework. Set up another appointment right then if the Holy

Spirit will allow you to. It reassures them they will be back and that you do care. People who are coming into your sessions need to have that peace and assurance. Many of them have never experienced the love of Christ and don't know that people can genuinely care for them. Comfort and love on them the way Jesus would.

HEALTH REASONS

When the Holy Spirit gives you the discernment to stop because of health reasons, listen! You don't know everyone's medical conditions and what is going on. If you are getting discernment the person's health is in danger, stop! When blood pressure and heart rates elevate too high or chest pains become an issue you need to be wise. For chest pains, they may feel some tightening or slight compression. If this is the case, I command the demons to leave and stop tormenting in Jesus' name. I then continue as released by the Holy Spirit. On occasion we have had to command blood pressure and heart rates to be normal in Jesus' name. No, we don't sit there with a blood pressure cuff on them. You know when people are getting tormented and have had too much. We stop, command their heart rate to be 80 beats per minute and their blood pressure to be 110/70. We will discretely take their pulse to make sure things have settled down or ask them if they are alright to go on. Take authority over demonic tormenting spirits and spirits of death. In most cases things settle down and we continue. I have only sent two people away due to health reasons.

ANGER AND VIOLENCE

We have full authority over anger and violent spirits. At the beginning of our session we command "There will be no anger or violence in Jesus' name." We have never experienced anger, violence or rage that we couldn't handle with the name of Jesus. I do suggest as you are first walking in this ministry, if you feel something rising and you don't know your full authority and are getting a little fearful, to close the session down and call in someone more experienced in your field. Always do deliverance with a team and be cautious. When the demons take over, the smallest child can become the strongest adult in their strength.

FATIGUE

When you or your client get worn out, frustrated and fatigued and you can't get past it you need to end the session. You have become ineffective to your team, the person you are ministering to and you can't effectively be used by God when you are overcome by feelings, tiredness and fatigue.

When we are done with a session we will advise the client if we feel they need more deliverance, follow up inner healing sessions, or if we feel the Lord is releasing them and finished with this season of deliverance. We then give them some follow up advice.

Follow up care to your deliverance session:

- We encourage them to come to our weekly or bi-weekly meetings so we can follow up with them, so they can be further equipped and held accountable. It assists them in staying clean, closing doors and moving forward.
- We make them aware the enemy could try and give them a little resistance in the coming weeks and lie to them that they are not free.
- Equip them if they feel anything attack them to simply say "Get away from me in Jesus' name."
- Encourage them to feel free to call or email the office with any questions or concerns.
- Advise them to pray before they talk to anyone about their deliverance. Not everyone believes in demons and many will not share in their excitement about what happened to them. Choose your conversations carefully.
- We then give them a prayer session follow up packet.

PRAYER SESSION FOLLOW UP PACKET

Upon completion of their session or the first session (if it is multiple sessions), we give our clients a prayer session follow up packet. These are handed out in a #10 envelope. In this envelope we have enclosed the following:

- FOLLOW UP LETTER - Located in the forms section of this book.

- TESTIMONIAL FORM - We believe in the blood of the Lamb and the word of our testimony. Written testimonies assist us in applying for grants. We can use them to show we are producing fruit in our ministry to other people interested in our services. It is also great for advertising on flyers, brochures and websites. We have them sign and agree to us using their testimony. They can also send a typed or emailed testimony into the ministry. (See a sample copy located in the forms section of this book.)

- PARTNERSHIP CARD - Our partnership card has a spot where they can partner with us financially on a monthly basis. We encourage them to sow into good ground. We also have a spot where they can sign up to receive weekly devotionals, be a prayer partner for us and hear about upcoming events.

- OFFERING ENVELOPE - We encourage people to give a love offering so we can continue to travel and provide resources for people in need.

- RETURN ENVELOPE - We enclose a return address envelope they can use for the testimony, partnership or love offering.

- BUSINESS CARDS - We enclose 3 business cards they can pass out to their friends who need deliverance, inner healing and/or mentoring. You can get free and inexpensive business cards and other stationary at www.vistaprint.com

- EVENT FLYERS - We enclose all our event flyers for meetings in their area and any upcoming meetings we want to encourage them to attend. We want to keep them plugged in and built up with good teaching and spirit filled believers.

We also enclose tools for building up the people in the following days after their session.

A booklet titled *Who I Am In Christ*. It is full of scriptures they are encouraged to read aloud 3 times daily to build them up. You can receive a sample copy of this booklet by visiting www.WhoIAmInChrist.net.

We also distribute to them a booklet called *Satan versus Christ,* which can be obtained free by visiting www.wmpress.org.

FEES

In order to have the greatest impact for the Kingdom of God we do not charge a fee for our sessions. Our ministry is supported by financial partners and love offerings from the general public. Many ministries charge a set fee for a deliverance or freedom session. We do not want to inhibit anyone from receiving the freedom they deserve. Christ freely gave us His freedom on the cross and we want to further extend that freely to the people we minister to. If you trust God, He will provide the financial needs for your ministry. Many times we have people walk into our sessions with checks already in their hands or amounts determined in their minds of what they want to financially sow into our ministry. They will bring you cash donations, checks, gift cards and even gifts. People are thankful for what you have done and many will automatically sow into your ministry. We encourage people to give financially to our ministry after the sessions. Upon completion of the sessions we hand people an offering envelope printed with our ministry information. This envelope can be separate from the prayer session follow up packet. We hand them the envelope and let them know that they can make an offering today or mail an offering in to further our ministry.

After a session you need to spiritually take care of your team. We do the following things at the end of each day of ministering.

Praise and worship God for what He did. We can do nothing by ourselves but everything with God's help. After defeating the enemy all day, we want to give praise and glory to God for all He has just done and put all the focus back on Him.

- Discern the atmosphere and make sure there is peace and not heaviness in the air.

- Pray off any attachments, defilements and transferences. We say "In Jesus' name we command any ungodly attachments, defilements or transferences to leave our bodies, the ministry center and our vehicles in Jesus' name."

- Discern yourself and those who ministered with you. Are you feeling good, do you have any body pain, are you feeling any heaviness? If so, pray off attachments again.

- Pray and give God the glory. We ask the Lord to come in and refresh us and refill us. Pray for the physical strength needed to get through the rest of the day.

- Pray protection for those who did deliverance and family members. Cancel any attacks of the enemy to steal, kill or destroy. We claim Is 54:17 "No weapon formed against you shall prosper, and every tongue which rises against you in judgment You shall condemn."

- Keep the focus on what God did and not the demonic realm. Don't go around talking about the demons and what happened. Give glory to God not the demonic.

- Be sensitive to any strong mood changes over the next couple of days and pray off any thing that might start to attack you.

At the end of the day, take a hot bath or go and soak in the river of life with Jesus Christ. Either way refresh, refill and just bask in His presence, I do!

The following are forms that we use in our ministry. Please feel free to adapt them to your personal needs.

Dear Friend in Christ,

Thank you for being obedient and allowing the Lord to use (name of your ministry) to assist you through a prayer session. We would like to give you some information about the attached forms as well as the process of our prayer sessions. We believe this will better equip you and our team in the process!

Attachments: *(The following should be completed and returned to the ministry.)*

- Prayer Sessions Questionnaire – this will better equip our team to know how to prepare and pray for you specifically when you arrive. It will assist in making the most efficient use of our time. (There is extra space on the blank page if necessary.)

- Legal Waiver – legally we are required to have each person attending a prayer session through (your ministry name) to read and sign this form.

Process:

- Upon completion of these forms, please return them to (your ministry name) using the self-address envelope enclosed, email or while you attend one of our gatherings.

- Once the application is received, we will pray over it and call you to schedule an appointment. Our usually office hours are (insert your office hours). We try to do this as quickly as possible, however, it can take up to a few weeks, and so please be patient with us!

- Prayer Session:

- Held at (your location).

- We will have 2 or 3 members of our team there to intercede for you. These are trusted team members that the Lord has chosen to be here. *Please understand that we have very strict confidentiality rules and nothing that is discussed in your prayer session will leave the room.* Please also know that a team will lead your session which may or may not include the founder of this ministry in on your session.

- Upon arrival we will sit down and discuss any questions we have about your application or developments you have had since filling out the application.
- We will then go into our prayer time of inner and spiritual healing.

We encourage you to complete these forms as honestly and directly as you can. Be assured the Lord will reveal to us what he needs us to know about you in order to help you obtain your freedom. Please begin to pray and ask the Holy Spirit to convict you of any unforgiveness you have in your life, healing you may need, and clarity during our session. In order to assist in your deliverance we suggest you fast in preparation for your session.

If you have any further questions, please feel free to e-mail us at (your email address) we look forward to praying with you in the future!

Whom the Son sets free is free indeed!

(ministry founders name), *Founder*

Your ministry name and/or logo and contact info.

Name: _____

Address: _____

City, State, Zip _____

Phone number _____

Email: _____

Referred by: _____

Date Recd _____

Date Scheduled _____

Best appt time   (insert days you minister)

CONFIDENTIAL DELIVERANCE QUESTIONAIRE

1. When were you born again, when did you accept Jesus as Lord? (year) _____

2. Have you been water baptized by immersion since your conversion? yes   no

3. Were you baptized in the Holy Spirit? (not the same as water baptism) If yes when? Year

4. Do you pray in tongues/in the spirit? yes   no

5. How would you describe your family's financial situation when growing up?

    Poverty   Stable   Comfortable

6. Do you consider yourself to be living in poverty now, have poverty income or government assistance? yes   no

7. Were you raised in a physically or emotionally abusive home?

    yes   no

Have you forgiven the person(s) yes no

8. Have you ever felt rejected, unloved by a relative, if so name relationship of relative(s)? yes no

Have you forgiven the person(s) yes no

9. Were you ever sexually abused, if yes how? yes no

molestation rape incest

Have you forgiven the person(s) yes no

10. Have you, your parents or spouse ever been involved in? (circle all that apply)
occult, witchcraft, Jehovah's witnesses, Mormons, freemasonry, Masonic lodges, shriners, elks clubs, job's daughters, Native religions, Islam, Christian Science, Scientology, cast spells, Satanism, spiritualist, eastern star

11. Have you ever had psychiatric counseling? yes no

12. Have you ever been hypnotized? yes no

13. Do you suffer from bad dreams or nightmares? yes no

14. Have you ever been tempted/tried to commit suicide? yes no

15. Have you ever wanted or attempted to kill someone? yes no

16. Have you ever had involvement with any of the following, including as a child? (circle all that apply)

fortunetellers, tarot cards, ouija boards, séances, mediums, soul ties, palm reading, astrology, horoscopes, lucky charms, black magic, dungeons and dragons, voodoo, yoga, eight ball, pendulum swinging, table tipping, levitation, crystals, clairvoyance, cast spells

17. Have you ever made a vow or oath to yourself or someone else?

yes no

18. Have you ever seen or felt a demonic presence? yes   no

19. Have you ever learned martial arts? yes   no

20. Do you have any tattoos, if yes what is it? yes   no

21. Have you ever been addicted to or had a problem with? (circle all that apply)

    drugs, gambling, spending, TV, alcohol, smoking, food, shopping, pornography, masturbation, compulsive exercise, caffeine (coffee or pop), chewing, chocolate, sugar, computer

22. Women only – have you ever had an abortion? yes   no

    Have you forgiven yourself? yes   no

23. Have you ever received prayer for deliverance? yes   no

    If yes, where and how

24. Did you have pre-marital sex? yes   no

25. Marital status (circle all that apply)-single, married, divorced, remarried, widowed

26. Have you committed adultery? yes   no

    If yes does your spouse know? yes   no

Please be truthful these questions remain confidential.

27. Are you holding unforgiveness against anyone? yes   no

28. Have you forgiven yourself for everything? yes   no

29. Do you get angry, out of control and/or yell? yes   no

30. Do you like to be in control? yes   no

31. Do you suffer from depression? yes   no

32. Are you a prideful person, battle with pride or have pride? yes no

33. Do you suffer from fear? If yes, what please circle all that apply and list any additional: confrontation, death, water, heights, dark, spouse leaving you, spouse or children dying, closed in spaces, insects, spiders, snakes, additional fears _____
_____

34. Have you ever experimented in homosexuality or had homosexual thoughts? yes   no

35. Do you have inappropriate (sexual) pictures/visions come to your mind? yes   no

36. Are you a perfectionist? yes   no

37. Are you a people pleaser? yes   no

38. Are you performance driven? yes   no

39. Are you complacent? yes   no

40. Have you lost a close loved one? yes   no

    Have you grieved?   yes   no

41. Do you strive – feel like you have to earn something/prove something? yes   no

42. Do you love yourself? Can you look in the mirror and say I love myself? yes   no

43. Have you or do you currently struggle with purging, bulimia and/ or anorexia? yes   no

44. Are you sick a lot? yes   no

45. Please list any health ailments you have been diagnosed by a doctor for or are on prescription medication.

46. Have you had any severe accidents or traumas that stand out in your mind not already mentioned about? Please explain:

Additional Notes:

<u>Please mail back to:</u>

(your ministry name and address)

<u>LEGAL WAIVER</u>

A sample copy of a Legal Waiver can be found in Doris Wagner's book *How to Cast Out Demons*.

Supplemental Deliverance Form (for follow up sessions)

Please fill out and return to: (your street address and email address)

Name: _____

Address: _____

Phone_____

City, State, Zip_____

Email_____

What church do you attend?_____

PRAYER NEED

_____
_____
_____
_____
_____
_____

REASON FOR FOLLOW UP VISIT

WHERE HAVEN'T YOU BEEN ABLE TO OBTAIN VICTORY?

_____
_____
_____
_____
_____
_____

Do you have a medical or clinical diagnosis from any physician, doctor, psychologist or counselor?

yes   no   If yes, please state diagnosis:_____

_____

_____

_____

_____

_____

LEGAL LIABILITY RELEASE

I, the undersigned do hereby release DeGraw Ministries and their volunteers or staff from any liability, for any harm or perceived harm resulting from my voluntary receiving of free prayer on this and subsequent visits. I understand that DeGraw Ministries is staffed by volunteers representing the Jesus Christ. They are not trained professionals of counseling, therapy of medical services. I understand that if I am currently taking medication, or operating under the advice of a professional service, I will allow them (my medical doctor, therapist, counselor, etc.) to confirm any results of prayer received before altering any prescribed course of action.

Signed:_____

 Date:_____

(Office Use: Date Recd: _____

Date Scheduled: _____

Notes: _____

Team in session: _____

DELIVERANCE NOTES -

Progress – changes since last visit:

_____

_____

_____

_____

_____

_____

Forgiveness still needed in the following areas:

_____

_____

_____

_____

_____

_____

Issues not resolved or to address in next session:

_____

_____

_____

_____

_____

_____

Spirits to revisit:

_____

_____

_____

_____

_____

_____

Dear Friend in Christ,

Thank you for choosing (your ministry name) for your inner healing and prayer session. We believe the Lord is using us in a mighty way to help set the captives free. We are honored to have been used by the Lord in such a way. He is the one who equips us for the ministry he has called us to.

In order to further our ministry and help in the follow up of your session please allow us to present to you the following information:

Follow up – In the days following your prayer session it can sometimes be challenging as the enemy tries to come in and "steal, kill and destroy, John 10:10" what the Lord just accomplished in your life. Remember the victory is in Jesus. However, victory comes with a price. We highly suggest and encourage you to stay with a spirit filled body of believers. We invite you to one of our gatherings "In His Presence". *See the enclosed card or website for details and location.*

Scriptures – You also need to confess and be praying the scriptures out loud over your life. Therefore, we have enclosed a "Who Am I in Christ" booklet to assist you.

In Luke 5:14 when Jesus had healed the leper Jesus said "But go and show yourself to the priest, and make an offering for your cleansing, as a testimony to them."

Testimony – Jesus said "Go and show yourself" and in Revelations it says "By the blood of the Lamb and the word of their testimony." Testimonies are important to growing our ministry and obtaining grants from corporations. Please prayerfully consider writing your testimony and returning it in the envelope provided (or you may email it). If can be as long or brief as you like. Please sign it – anonymous, with your initials, first name or full name.

Offering – Jesus said "Make an offering for your cleansing." We do not charge for our services, however, we want to be obedient to the Lord. If he is calling you to make a love or thank offering you can receive a tax deductible receipt. Your money will allow us to purchase books and continue traveling to help people in future prayer sessions and to further advance our ministry.

If you have any further prayer needs please feel free to email them to:

(Your intercessors email address) they will gladly stand in agreement with you in prayer.

Blessings and enjoy walking in victory!

(founders name) and deliverance team!

Founder

DELIVERANCE GUIDELINES

Thank you for opening up your home and allowing us to minister to people in your region.

We appreciate your willingness to help set the captives free.

It is our desire to minister to the people you send our way in the most effective way possible so they will receive freedom in Christ and a deeper intimacy with Him. We also desire to pour into you so that you can grow in your walk and also be equipped for all the ministry that God has for you. In order to do this we need to carefully schedule the time we have while with you. For us to fulfill these two desires we ask that the following guidelines be adhered to in advance and while ministering in your area.

- All people interested in a deliverance session must fill out a form and mail back or email back to (your ministry name) in (state) prior to departure of trip.
- Once the form has been received by (your ministry name), we will review, pray over the form and schedule an appointment if applicable before departure to your region.
- All deliverances must be scheduled through (your ministry name) via phone or email prior to arriving in your region.
- For the effectiveness of deliverances, the freedom of the people and the spiritual and physical well being of the (your ministry name) we will need to be in control of scheduling all deliverances through our offices in (state).

As a team, we want to stay in good physical and spiritual shape while we are with you so that we can give our all to each person that we minister to including you! For us to be able to stay in the best shape possible, please take into consideration the following:

- We need down time.
- We need to be able to rest and refill between sessions.

- We need to be able to hear from the Lord and not be fatigued or overwhelmed with a schedule.
- We need time to be in prayer and worship.
- We know how long sessions will last and how much time we need between each.
- We cannot give people our best if we are over booked and burned out.
- We need time to sow and minister to our hosts.

We kindly ask that while in your region you do not insist on us "fitting one more in." We cannot always do it and while there are extreme cases we will always take it to prayer and ask you to accept the direction the Lord gives. Please remember, it isn't always a person's time. The enemy can also use deliverances to distract us from what we are really supposed to be doing.

Thank you again for your respect and consideration to our service to the Lord. We are always trying to increase and improve in his direction and we appreciate you helping us be obedient!

If you have any questions about the above information, please call the ministry office or e-mail your questions to (your email address).

(Your ministry name) Deliverance Team Application

Name: _____

Address: _____

Phone: _____ Cell:_____

Email: _____

Church Currently Attending: _____

What are you doing to grow your spiritual walk?

How would you describe your intimacy and relationship with Jesus Christ?

Do you pray in tongues daily? yes   no   if no, how often or not at all? _____

Who is your spiritual mentor? _____ How often do you meet? _____

Who is your accountability partner? _____ How often do you meet?_____

Have you read the book *The Bait of Satan* by John Bevere? yes no

(recommended reading for our ministry workers)

Do you get offended easily? yes   no

Can you take direction easily? yes   no

Do you desire to be in your own ministry? yes   undecided   no

Why have you chosen to learn about deliverance ministry?

What are your intentions with (your ministry name) deliverance - check all that apply

- ☐ Observe and learn for whatever the Lord is calling me to
- ☐ Be part of your intercession team in deliverance sessions
- ☐ Assist you and do hands on deliverance
- ☐ Be able to be certified with credentials from (your ministry name)
- ☐ Be available to travel with (your ministry name) as my schedule and the Lord allows
- ☐ Start my own deliverance teams
- ☐ Be mentored by (your ministry name)

Why should we consider you to be part of our teams?

What days and times are you available for deliverance sessions from the following?

(Specify the time slots you are going to schedule sessions for your ministry.)

Have you received deliverance prayer? no yes - by what ministry

It is the policy of the ministry that you must have received a deliverance session by (your ministry name) in order to serve on the deliverance teams as a participant, team member or intercessor.

(Your ministry name)

TESTIMONIAL

Please complete and return this form to:

Your ministry name   or   your ministry name
Ministry address   (your ministry email address)

What God has done for me:

_____
_____
_____
_____
_____
_____
_____
_____
_____
_____

(your name)

Please circle one of the following below:

Yes, you may use part of or all of my testimony to declare the works of the Lord (only first names will be used).

No, please do not publicly use any part of my testimony

ABOUT THE AUTHOR

Kathy DeGraw is the founder and president of DeGraw Ministries, a healing and deliverance ministry. She strengthens, teaches, trains and equips believers to experience the fullness of God! She has a clear and unique gift of discernment and operates in a strong healing and deliverance anointing. She believes in calling forth the glory of the Lord to heal, set free and deliver!

Kathy stretches believers to reach for more so they can be equipped for the ministry God is calling them to. She is passionate about establishing other ministries in order to have more people advancing the Kingdom of God and setting the captives free. She believes in breaking down religious and denominational barriers and in her weekly meetings equips believers to live a spirit filled life and transform their churches.

She is passionate about worship and intimacy with the Lord and believes the Lord is rising up a new generation of worshipers who will worship Him in freedom, spirit and truth. She believes spending time with the Lord on the floor prostrate seeking His face is the key to intimacy and relationship with Him. She teaches women how to go from pew sitters to worshipers and strengthen their relationship with Christ.

Kathy is the author of "The Sky's the Limit". How to create an amazing Kids Club outreach program to reach out to the children in your community and grow your church. She has received the American Author's Association, 2009 Golden Quill Award for The Sky's the Limit.

Kathy and her husband, Ron, have three teenage children, Dillon, Amber, and Lauren and make their home in Grandville, Michigan.

To book Kathy for a speaking engagement or deliverance school in your area contact;

DeGraw Ministries
P.O. Box 65
Grandville, Michigan 49468
Website: www.degrawministries.org
Email: admin@degrawministries.org

ALSO BY KATHY DEGRAW

THE SKY'S THE LIMIT – Creating an Amazing Kids Club
Published by CSS Publishing
ISBN 0-7880-2561-9

Do you have the desire to create or expand your church's ministry to children, but don't know where to start? **The Sky's the Limit** offers valuable insight into how to create a kids' club in your church where children can not only have fun, but also learn more about God and grow in their Christian faith. Although the idea of starting a children's ministry may seem overwhelming, **The Sky's the Limit** takes you step by step through the process to ensure a smooth transition for both children and teachers.

Drawing from her own experience, Kathy DeGraw guides ministry leaders in every aspect of the creation of a kids' club – from assembling a ministry team to choosing snack ideas to creating fun activities, and so on.

According to DeGraw, having a kids' club can be a powerful evangelistic outreach, because by reaching out to the children in your community, you are also reaching out to their entire families, drawing them not only into your church, but into a relationship with God.

In taking this first step to establishing a children's ministry in your church, the sky truly is the limit on the impact you can have in your community!

Lightning Source UK Ltd.
Milton Keynes UK
UKOW051129061112

201749UK00010B/170/P